# Woman's Magic

# Woman's Magic

### Rituals, meditations, and magical ways to enrich your life

## Sue Bowes

☥ WEISER BOOKS

York Beach, Maine, USA

*In loving memory of Justin Carson*

Weiser Books, Inc.
P. O. Box 612
York Beach, ME 03910-0612
*www.weiserbooks.com*

Library of Congress Cataloging-in-Publication Data

Bowes, Susan.
    Woman's Magic : rituals, meditations, and magical ways to enrich
your life / Sue Bowes
        p. cm.
    Includes bibliographical references and index
    ISBN 1-57863-221-8 (pbk. : alk. paper)
        1. Witchcraft.  2. Magic.  3. Ritual.  4. Goddess religion.  I. Title.
    BF1566 .B675 2001
    133.4'3'082—dc21                                    00-047229

Typeset in 11/15 Bembo
Cover design by Kathryn Sky-Peck

Printed in the United States of America
VG

09  08  07  06  05  04  03  02  01
10  9  8  7  6  5  4  3  2  1

*Woman's Magic* is dedicated to Geb, Lord of the
Earth and to man's magic because without it
woman's magic would be a mere flicker.

Look well to this day
for it is life —
the very best of life
In its brief course
lie all the realities and truths
of existence
The joy of growth,
the splendour of action,
the glory of power

For yesterday is but a memory
and tomorrow is but a vision
But today, if well lived,
makes every yesterday
a memory of happiness
and every tomorrow
a vision of hope
Look well therefore to this day

*Ancient Sanskrit poem*

# Acknowledgements

A huge thanks to everyone at Gaunts House, especially to
Daphne, Kamini, Bodi Prem, and to Markie-Larkie, Clare, Julia
and Andrew – the mad kitchen cooks; but above all to Richard
for being such a great friend and support. . .
. . . and to all of you who are drawn to reading this book.

# Contents

# Introduction

ACROSS THE WORLD TODAY many women are being drawn back to the old ways of following the patterns of nature as part of their daily routine both at home and at work. These people are not witches, in the sense of the wicked witch of the north, nor are they particularly interested in cavorting around naked in the moonlight. Neither are they ardent feminists. They are ordinary women like you and me who simply wish to acknowledge the magical power of the feminine as equal to that of the masculine. The balance between the masculine and the feminine (or *yin* and *yang* as it is known in Eastern esoteric terms) is a finite law in the universe. When an imbalance occurs it creates chaos. I do not have to explain how this havoc manifests. We wake up to it and live in the midst of it every day.

The aim of *Woman's Magic*, therefore, is to inspire women not just to reconnect with their innate inner magic but also to reclaim it. This is the essence of femininity; and it is her femininity (as opposed to sexuality) which makes a woman so special and mysterious. The pace of modern life does little to support or encourage the practice of the old ways, and too many of us find ourselves out of touch with our own quintessence and therefore at a loss to know how to use our inherent feminine wiles and wisdom to their full potential. If we are to take our places in society as fully integrated women, it is important for us to learn how to rekindle the magic for our own health and inner contentment, as well as using it for the benefit of all those with whom we come into contact.

## My Healing Path

I began my own healing path after surviving a plane crash. At the time my life was a mess; I was in a perpetual state of anxiety and unhappiness, and working in an area which did little to fulfil me. It happened on a beautiful sunny August evening. We were about three-quarters of an hour into the flight at around 2,000 feet when the propeller stopped going round. At first I thought it was the pilot trying to impress me, but when I saw the colour drain from his face, I knew it was serious. He immediately sent out a mayday call, and began to try to find somewhere to put the plane down. In the meantime, I went into an altered state of being. I felt like I could finally give up my life of struggle. The feeling was an overwhelming 'Thank God it's all over.' In my head, I said goodbye to everyone I could think of, and opened myself up to receive my death with resignation. With that we hit trees, and catapulted into a field. Everything went into slow motion; I can remember the whole plane disintegrating around us, and the windscreen exploding into me. I also remember praying for the end to be quick. Yet within seconds I realised that I was very much alive and scrambling to get out of the wreck because it was in danger of blowing up. I remember sitting on the grass in complete shock and outrage that I had lived. My depression was so bad that for the next few weeks I could barely drag myself out of bed. Everything was a shambles and, being incapable of work, financial disaster was also looming. Yet destiny had another card to play which was to completely change my life. One afternoon I found myself lying on the sofa, in complete despair. I had no idea what to do, where to go, or who to talk to, when suddenly it was as if a sentence dropped into my head from above. It said quite simply: 'You will become a bereavement counsellor.' I sat bolt upright. Of course! That is what I had been looking for all my life – an avenue of work which meant something, which could help me as well as other people. From that moment on I began to live. I trained as a bereavement counsellor which enabled me to deal with my own unresolved grief issues, and from there I began to work in service for the 'greater good'. This in turn led me to write my first book, *Notions and Potions*, which opened the door to really exploring the great mysteries of life. Even so it took an enormous jump to finally walk my talk.

## Meeting with the Power of the Divine Goddess

This meant making the ultimate surrender to the Goddess energy. I would talk about her a lot, and happily took part in Goddess rituals, but to actually surrender to her, that was another matter altogether. It frightened me to death because, in the back of my mind, I felt that if I was to do this my whole life would suddenly come to an end as I knew it. Would I have to give up that glass of wine, or lounging in the sun, or all those other luxuries which make life so affable? Would surrendering to the Goddess mean an end to all this? It was during a particularly powerful meditation that I finally 'got' it. I realised that life is about being in complete service to the divine – call it God, the Goddess, the Great Creator or whatever feels comfortable to you. Nothing else really matters. Unless we enter into this service, our lives are like empty shells in which we bounce chaotically from wall to wall, causing havoc in everything we do. This, however, does not mean that we have to give up our little luxuries either if they make us feel happy and content. Piety, suffering, self-abuse, abstinence, wearing hair shirts or whipping yourself to death is not part of serving the Goddess nor the greater good. To spread joy, you need to feel joy, and 'en-joy' what you love to do. We are fortunate in the Western world to have the resources to cushion ourselves against the need to fight for survival. As long as we are respectful of what we own, and maintain a healthy, balanced attitude towards what we really need, how we earn our keep and honour our own personal integrity, we can realise how blessed we are, and give thanks for it too.

I wanted to find a ring, a special silver 'Goddess' ring to wear as a symbol of my commitment or surrender to her. I found it in a jewellery shop and it slipped on to my finger as if it had been made especially for me. I then conducted a special dedication or baptism by the ocean. First I called on the devic forces to bear witness to what I was doing, then took the ring, and blessed it in the sea – and then offered it to the Goddess. I surrendered my soul to her service and, as the sun began to set, put the ring on. I knew there was no going back. It was probably one of the most sacred and holy moments of my life.

I wear my ring constantly as a reminder that the Goddess is literally always 'on hand'. If things get a bit rough, it is there to remind me that I need to let go and allow her to do the work. She knows best even if the circumstances appear to be confusing or frightening. In addition, my true force seems to be coming alive, and I know at long last I am on the right path. I am doing what I love to do, and loving what I do. I have also lost my fear of the unknown. I live much more in the present, dealing with matters which are in front of my nose rather expending energy and time worrying about what may or may not happen in an uncertain future. I also feel safe within myself, even though it seems that the rest of the world is on the brink of destruction. I realise that the support I can give to the world is to be ruthless about my own personal integrity, and to work as a channel of light in whatever way I can. Sometimes this is as simple as lighting a candle to all those poor souls who are helpless and homeless. No one can save the world single-handed, but we can hold the energy of positive power and lead by example.

This was how I made my commitment to the Goddess. You may want to do it in a completely different way, or indeed you may feel this is not for you. Your spiritual commitment is a profoundly personal journey, and one that needs time and reflection. It is not something to be taken lightly. Once we open the door to the higher forces, it is as if the floodgates of our soul burst. In order to be a carrier for the light, our negative programming also has to be resolved. It is not an easy path to tread because we have to enter into something which more often than not feels like the pits of hell. All the women I know who have done this have had to face all kinds of debilitating loss as well as the terror of looking into the eyes of insanity. But once the light does begin to shine, there is a different feel to life, and a profound knowing that you are making a difference just by being alive.

My learning has also led me to explore my psyche. I am constantly amazed at what it comes up with, and the guidance it provides, especially through the archetypes (for more on these, have a look at Chapter 6) which manifest in my mind with such reality that they have become like old friends. Whenever I am confused or lost, I go inside and ask the feeling to transform into an archetype which then provides me with the answers I need to break through the negative and turn it into the positive. I also communicate with them just for fun or if I'm bored. Personal growth does not mean that we have to be intensely navel gazing all the time. In the end, it's about building an integrated relationship with yourself so you can laugh at your foibles and mad idiosyncratic behaviour with the pure joy of being you! No one else is you or ever will be. That, in itself, is quite a thought.

This magical inner archetypal realm broadened my

self-knowledge to such an extent that I wanted to share the experience with other people – and so the concept of *Woman's Magic* was born.

*Woman's Magic* is a practical, updated *grimoire* (or book of magical recipes, rituals and incantations) showing how easy and pleasurable it is to incorporate the age-old ways of the wise woman into the demanding life of any contemporary woman. It ranges from exploring sexual archetypes, to harmonising the home and pepping up culinary delights, to planting and harvesting, and understanding the influence of astrological and numerological cycles. It also underlines the importance of supporting each other by forming ongoing sisterhoods and exploring new ways of working in harmony with each other. I do want to emphasise, however, that this is not a book about magical spells. It is to do with feminine ritual magic which brings back the meaning of respect, appreciation and reverence into a world which has all but forgotten the significance of it.

## The Importance of Ritual

Ritual work is also important in woman's magic. Ritual is for focusing the mind, for making something sacred and sacrosanct. It enables you to open your heart so communication can take place with your inner self. This is where your ultimate truth lies; from where you receive inspiration, visions, and those sixth sense knowings. It is that part of yourself which is yours and yours alone. To be fully functional and for it to develop, it needs to be exercised, just as your body does. Ritual work enables this to happen and begins to tame our wild imagination so it becomes a source of incredible symbology which leads us further and further along our path of self-knowledge. This is where our archetypes also reside. It is through communication with them that we can glean a vivid understanding of how we feel about ourselves. I believe that as we communicate more and more with all the different facets of our inner selves, our outer lives support this through extraordinary coincidences and synchronicities. It is as if these archetypes are out there too. I had a particularly astonishing experience of this myself.

I had been working on my archetypal priestess image, and what she meant to me. I finally met her in my inner realms as a powerful snake goddess which prompted some thought. The snake has always caused me a lot of consternation because I have always been frightened and repulsed by them. However, it did mean something to me because nine years previously I attended a workshop where, unbeknown to me, snakes were to play an important part in an initiation ceremony. I couldn't believe my eyes when I saw them entwined on their snake handlers. The only way I got through was to close my eyes and pray! I then felt one being gently pushed up my trouser leg. I cannot describe the feeling of terror, but I knew if I moved, it would probably bite me, so I became paralysed. The second time the snake was placed on me, I suddenly felt an overwhelming feeling of sorrow for it. Poor little thing being pushed around like this. Although I still wasn't able to open my eyes, something shifted. After that, I adopted a respectful attitude towards them and found that I could allow them to enter into my life a little more fully.

After meeting my inner snake priestess, snake symbology began to play quite a large role in my life, particularly during a visit to Crete. On my last day, together with a friend, I visited Knossos, the famous snake temple. As I leant against one of its walls, I had an overwhelming feeling that I had been part of the temple at one stage and this had been a mighty place full of the mystical and magical powers of women. I could almost see the snakes, and feel them entwined around my body. I then became consumed with a deep horror and grief about the desecration that this holy place suffered under the feet of thousands of gaping visitors who hadn't got a clue. I also felt an intense disgust that the temple complex had disintegrated into a mere money spinner. We left within minutes.

Later that day, my friend and I arrived at the airport to fly home. I had a strong instinct to go and wait on a bench outside rather than be surrounded by itinerant passengers. As I sat down on one of the benches, I glanced behind me, and there, propped up against the wall, was a long walking stick of staff length. It was made of cane, but the most extraordinary thing was that its head was in the shape of a snake. As I took hold of it, my friend spluttered: 'My God, that's your priestess staff!' We were both completely shaken by this, and totally mystified as to how it came to be there. Naturally it came home with me.

A couple of weeks later, I attended a workshop on the integration of mind, body and spirit. We were given a lucky dip, and guess what I drew out – a cuddly snake! One of the facilitators commented out of the blue: 'Oh look, that's your priestess power totem.' Get the idea? Be prepared for things like this to occur in your life too.

## Taking Responsibility for the Heavenly Forces within

The origin of humankind has always been a contentious issue. Most scientists are in agreement that we have evolved from the oceans. Yet virtually every ancient culture embraced the belief that their ancestry was intermingled with beings from different parts of the galaxy, and these beings were known as the 'gods'. (The word *god* comes from the Sanskrit root g*hu* meaning to worship). There is plenty of evidence to support this. It can be seen in the hieroglyphs on the walls of many of the ancient sacred sites found in central and South America and the Middle East, and also in the cave drawings of Aboriginals. Perhaps it was these gods who provided the mathematical knowledge to erect such fabulous intricate structures. Today, with all our modern technological knowhow, we still don't know how the Pyramids of Egypt were constructed, nor how Stonehenge was built.

Even the Bible alludes to some kind of union between the heavens and humankind. In Genesis (5:2) it says: *Then the sons of God saw the daughters of man and they were fair; And they took wives of all which they chose.* It is interesting that the Bible refers to the 'sons of God', while women are described as 'daughters of man'. Christian teachings were rigorous in maintaining the value of woman as lower than that of men. In any case, all the ancient mythological traditions, no matter their origins, refer to the heavens as being a source, or seat, of some kind of super intelligence represented in male *and* female form which influenced the destiny of humankind. Before Christianity took hold in Europe, the essences of the god and goddess were regarded as equal. Massive temple complexes were created to honour them, and great festivals were held to celebrate their might. Shrines were also an integral part of every household, and homage was paid to individual gods and goddesses as a daily routine to ask for favours, blessings and forgiveness, as well as for appeasement!

The Christian church was very quick to stamp out this practise and to corrupt the dual force into the semblance of an all-seeing and all knowing vengeful God - without a goddess in sight. It became obligatory for worship to take place in a 'house of God' under the watchful eye of an officiating male priest while women's roles in the scriptures were reduced to the stark duality of the virgin or whore. This Christian God was to do with suffering, a male force which had the power to cast a disobedient soul in the depth of hell with one swoop of his hand. Guilt was indoctrinated into the population through the hellfire and brimstone teachings of the pulpit and the rigid practice of confession. Fear of terrible retribution took away people's ability to think for themselves, or to follow their own inner wisdom, and this was passed down mercilessly from generation to generation together with the image of women as tainted, and subservient to men. The consequence of this brainwashing led to a gross imbalance in society, as well as insidiously robbing women of their sense of worth. It's been a long battle to redress this balance, and it is still going on.

I believe that the ancient religions were right. I believe that the heavens are a source of some kind divine masculine and feminine power - the god *and* goddess – which connects with the very soul of who we are. I'm not sure if we have evolved from beings from other galaxies, but I am sure that an extraordinary power and innate knowledge is impregnated into every one of us at a cellular level, and we are able to tap into this source at any moment we choose because *as above, so below; as without, so within.* We are a part of all things in the universal consciousness just as all things in the universal consciousness are a part of us. Our ancient ancestors understood this, and devoutly focussed on images of gods and goddesses as a way of paying homage to the awesome force of a duality which they believed guided their way. They realised that without the infinite balance of the masculine and feminine both internally and externally, the world would destroy itself.

Spiritual development is about the journey which takes you to your own inner heaven where your personal god and goddess reside, the animus and anima. In this sense, you are the living embodiment of universal god and the goddess and therefore *you are your own divine creators.* This means that no matter how ordinary you feel your life to be, or that your body is weak or even impaired – YOU MATTER. You are doing your ultimate divine work by staying in a state of loving awareness. Through this action, you are contributing to the progress of humanity which can only take another step forward in its consciousness when enough of us begin to deal with aggression with love, understanding, peace and above all, forgiveness. By becoming a living example of divine harmony – without pushing it down people's throats – those who are still groping around in the dark are given the opportunity of seeing that there is indeed another way, and that the world is a truly magical place. Reverent love has an energy all of its own. It can walk through walls and heal the deepest wounds. It will also be the salvation of the world, and when this happens I sincerely hope that we will once again accept images of gods and goddesses as powerful religious and spiritual icons.

## Woman's Magic, the Earth, the Goddess – and Sex

In early times, woman was regarded as the sacred and magical vessel through which the gods from the heavens could manifest life on earth. There are numerous indigenous creation myths and legends which also tell of the unity between woman and the gods as part of the evolutionary process of humankind. Many stories include the concept that the gods mated with woman in the disguise of an animal, for example the rape of Leda by Zeus disguised as a swan. The theme of woman and beast being brought together for the development of human life was central to the now extinct Mandan tribe of North America. They believed that humankind had descended from a sexual union between bison and woman. The woman absorbed the essence of the animal to provide the spirit of bison knowledge and power for her people, thus ensuring their survival.

A woman's magic was associated with the mysterious ways of the earth because it was woman who gave life just as the earth provided life for all living things. Likewise, herbal lore was traditionally associated with woman's magic principally because it was they who tended to the plants and crops while their men were out hunting. Medicinal remedies and secret magical potions were passed down orally from mother to daughter for generations. 'Woman' was therefore very much regarded as a representative on earth of the divine feminine; the Goddess herself.

It is known that virtually all the ancient religions around the world were based on goddess worship which centred around either the earth or the moon. Great temples were built in her honour and many effigies were made of a goddess depicted as a fertility symbol with large childbearing hips and succulent breasts. Voluptuous sexuality was the major part of her symbology, and many ceremonies throughout the year, which were marked by the solstices and equinoxes, incorporated powerful fertility rituals to ensure the continuation of humanity, beast and crops.

The role of priestess was central to ancient magical fertility rites. The oldest hymn (originally hymns were festive songs) dates back to the 3rd millennium BC from the land of Sumer. It is the tale of the Goddess Inanna calling out: 'Who will plough my vulva? Who will plough my wet ground?' This is answered by her brother Dumuzzi who is also her lover: 'I, Dumuzzi the King, will plough your vulva.' This heavenly symposium guaranteed the fruitfulness of the land during harvest. The Sumerians enacted this conjugation through a mystical marriage between their own king and a priestess from the Temple of the Goddess Inanna. This mystical marriage was widely known by its Greek name of *hieros gamos*. At the point of their union, it was considered that the king and priestess became the physical embodiments of these two divinities, thus bringing the divine energies of the Goddess and God into earthly matter. It is possible that *hieros gamos* were practised before Sumerian times, but the earliest records were found in the shrines of Anatolia which date back to around 6,000 BC. These practices, together with the powerful personification of the priestess, were celebrated and revered throughout the Middle East and all over Europe right up until the rise of the Christian church.

# The Attempted Destruction of Woman's Magic

The Christian fathers attempted to obliterate the role of priestess and any reference to woman's magic. Any woman found practising the old crafts was immediately labelled a witch which automatically brought the death penalty usually after appalling torture to gain confession. It has been suggested that as many as three million so-called witches may have been put to death during the Dark Ages, the last being in Germany in 1775. These 'witches' were, in the main, herbalists, teachers, midwives and women who lived alone without the protection of a man. The persecutions stopped as a result of public outcry at the loss of so many sisters, daughters, mothers, aunts and grandmothers.

So, according to history, legend and myth, a woman's magic has always been inexplicably bound up with enchantment, seduction, enigma, intrigue and rather a lot of mayhem – and very little appears to have changed!

## The Cycle of Giving and Receiving

I want to end this introduction by saying a few words about the cycle of giving and receiving. A truly magical life can only be accomplished by entering into the universal symmetry of giving and receiving as an equality. To take without wanting to give something back represents a deep fear of lack. To give without being willing to receive represents a destructive low self-worth.

It is also vital to practise gratitude as a daily ritual. Being grateful for what we have, no matter how small it is, delivers us straight into the universal flow of manifestation. To help with this, I have included in Chapter 2 a wonderful ritual for making a tree of gratitude which you can easily follow.

# WOMAN'S MAGIC

*Woman's Magic* is divided into seven chapters. I chose seven specifically since seven is one of the numbers of the moon, as well as of magic. Each chapter covers an area which immediately affects our lives: our sexuality, our home and workplace, the garden, special occasions, our spiritual development, our relationship with the Goddess, and lastly with each other. Every chapter contains powerful ritual meditations which will help you to access your inner wisdom, as well as providing relevant magical information you can incorporate simply into your daily life. Practising woman's magic is about being fully conscious of who you are and taking responsibility for what you create rather than manufacturing some supersonic ceremony with neon lights and flashing symbols. In fact, in my own experience, the more simple the ritual, the more effective it becomes.

I trust that, by the end of the book, you will have a far deeper understanding of who you are and what you are capable of as a woman filled with your own brand of magic. Just remember to keep an open loving heart as you practise and experiment with your magic – and nothing can go wrong!

I do hope that you enjoy making full use of *Woman's Magic*. I also hope that it will inspire you to inspire other women you meet along your path. Woman's magic is special, and so are you.

# Chapter 1
# Woman's Magic
# in Sexuality

Woman's magic means
not being a man!

*Daphne Archard*

**A** WOMAN'S MAGIC IS INTRICATELY entwined with her sexuality, and it is this mystical and nebulous combination which can cause an abstemious man to drink, send a sane man mad and make a grown man cry. To understand why, it is important to grasp the historical progression of women's sexual role in society which reaches back to the origins of survival. The influence of these women, the abuse they took and what happened to them is still alive in our genetic make-up because, whether we are aware of it or not, they are our ancestors. Woman's sexuality is, in essence, inspiration – the literal translation of which means *to breathe spirit*. When a woman is in full control of her body, mind and emotions, and has opened her heart to the call of her spirit, she becomes the embodiment of the divine female principle through which a man can reach ecstatic states. He knows this somewhere deep inside, and therefore is subconsciously always on the hunt for that ultimate experience which can only be found through mystical union with a woman. This belief forms the basis of all Eastern religions which stem back thousands and thousands of years.

Unfortunately, because of the way that Western society has metamorphosed predominantly through the hell-fire and brimstone attitude of Christianity, most women are so out of touch with their divine feminine that all sorts of problems ensue. So it is through gaining sagacity of our sexual heritage that we can not only begin to enjoy our selves as rounded women in contemporary life, but also to have some fun with it. To do this, we need to find the archetypes of our female ancestors who live in the recesses of our hearts and minds, and to embrace them as part of ourselves. We also need to learn to pay homage to that *circumambulating aphrodisiac* (in the words of Christopher Fry) the threefold vision of the moon, because it is she who regulates our body cycles as well as our emotional ups and downs, and guides us in our dream time. However, before we enter into the arcane world of the moon, let's explore our connection with the earth.

## Gaia, the Great Provider

In ancient times the world was considered to be feminine in essence and therefore extremely lascivious as well as contrary. In Western mythology she was given the name Gaia – which is taken from the Greek *goddess of the earth*. It is said that Gaia was born immediately after chaos and just before Eros, and that says it all! To those who held life as sacred, Gaia was a living, conscious entity, creating a holistic opportunity for man and beast to thrive in unison. She also created opportunity for destiny and consciousness to metamorphose through the evolutionary and sexual process of humankind. Therefore the earth and her feminine idiosyncrasies was an intrinsic part of man's mystical and spiritual experiences. The world was the great goddess, the mother, provider and nurturer, as well as the ferocious destroyer who required unremitting appeasement, and this belief was shared by all the great civilisations of bygone times.

# WOMAN'S MAGIC IN SEXUALITY

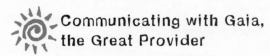 ## Communicating with Gaia, the Great Provider

### SETTING UP AT HOME

This ritual cries out for physical contact with nature, but you can adapt it in the comfort of your home. Should this be your choice, go out into nature first and find a small branch which has dropped from a tree, or collect a bundle of twigs and leaves, or perhaps some fresh flowers and herbs from the hedgerow. If this is not possible you can use a potted plant or put a bunch of flowers into a vase to represent Gaia. Create an altar – or a special sacred space on a table which you can decorate with pictures of the earth together with either the things you have gathered outside, or a potted plant or vase of flowers, and light a green candle in honour of her. You could also play a tape of bird songs softly in the background to help to create the right atmosphere.

### SETTING UP IN NATURE

Make sure you dress appropriately, depending on the weather! During mediation your body temperature drops, so make sure you take something warm to wrap up in. Find a place in nature where you feel safe and at ease, and somewhere where you will not be disturbed. I usually sit under a favourite tree or go to the local river. Maybe you have a favourite spot in your garden.

Working with nature means entering into the rhythm and cycle of giving and receiving, so take something you can leave as an offering of thanks such as food, herbs or tobacco when you finish. Spend a few minutes before you begin finding items which represent the magic of the earth to you such as leaves, twigs, flowers or stones. Place these

with your offering on the ground where you have chosen
to be.

## PREPARING YOURSELF

Close your eyes, and breathe out any tensions in your
body. Scan your body with your mind's eye and see where
these tensions may be. As you become more relaxed start
to feel the ground beneath you, and perhaps the trunk of
the tree supporting you. Take a few moments to enjoy the
sounds of the birds, the water passing by and the insects in
the grass. Feel the power and magnitude of Gaia surrounding and supporting you. Allow her to become part of you
as you are part of her. Notice how you feel about what you
are doing. What thoughts are passing through your mind?
Just allow yourself to be exactly how you are and gently let
go into the process.

Take yourself deeper into your inner realms and,
when you feel ready, call out to Gaia, the Great Provider,
to make herself known to you. Ask her to show you both
sides of herself: the mother, provider and nurturer as well as
the ferocious destroyer. Notice what feelings and emotions
begin to arise as you witness her. Work with any feelings of
fear by breathing them out of your body and releasing
them into the earth. When you feel ready, begin a dialogue
with her. See what comes. It could be a vision, or feelings
or indeed words in your head. Sometimes nothing makes
sense or perhaps you doubt the validity of what you are
doing. Just keep going. Each time you make a connection
with her, it will become stronger, and more things will
make sense.

Ask her for guidance about what kind of service you
can do for the benefit of the planet as well as for yourself.
Offer yourself to her, and make a vow that you are

prepared to dedicate yourself to helping to heal her in whatever way is appropriate in your life. This could be anything from simply deciding to pick up litter on the side of the road to joining Greenpeace. By becoming conscious of her needs, you are entering into, and adding to, the earth's much needed healing process.

When you feel complete, and at peace with yourself, open your eyes. Take a few moments to give gratitude to the earth. By making this a daily habit in one way or another, you become much more connected with her. Allow the power of the earth to seep into your psyche because, without a strong sense of Gaia within yourself, it is difficult to maintain your centre as a powerful, integrated woman. The connection with Gaia provides a rooted foundation, a feeling of being solidly placed upon the earth, of being supported by it. From this stance you can cope with all the things that happen in life, because Gaia is forever there, providing you with all you need. Once you are ready to leave, scatter the offering that you brought on the earth. You can also say a short prayer, or read a poem or saying which is special to you. It is also advisable to write down what you have experienced and to keep a record of any ritual you perform. By doing this, you can see how your inner vision changes over time, and how you deepen the connection with yourself, and that of your environment.

## CALLING ON GAIA TO HELP WITH HEALING

Whenever you have been knocked off the rails by some emotional trauma, or are consumed with loneliness, as soon as you can, go into nature and connect with Gaia. Give her your sorrow and grief, tell her your problems and ask for her help. Sometimes it can help to dig a small hole and then speak or shout your woes or illnesses into it. The hole then can be covered up. Many shamanic traditions practise this as a powerful method of healing.

The more you communicate with Gaia, the more you also link with your own core. By doing this, it begins to heal the separation that everyone feels within, and you no longer feel so alone.

# The Priestess

The role of priestess as the representation of the Goddess was entwined with her sexuality and this infiltrated virtually all ancient cultures throughout the world in one way or another. Paying for a temple priestess in the time-honoured traditions of *hieros gamos* meant of course that her 'guest' could achieve divine status. The priestess would place her payment on the altar which would accumulate in time to secure her release. In fact, during the Babylonian ceremony of renewal which took place around the winter solstice, it was essential for the present king to undergo *hieros gamos* with a priestess to justify his rule, and to act as an assurance that he possessed the sexual prowess and fertility required for the land, and therefore his people, to prosper.

The spirit of *hieros gamos* was also enacted during the advent of spring, where huge festivals were held to celebrate the time for new life to spring forth. In many communities, a young man and woman would be selected to represent the divine duality of male and female to mark the beginning of the season. The young male hunter represented the Horned God of Virility; the young female symbolised fecundity of Earth Mother. A great hunt took place where the prowess and suitability of the Horned God would be tested through his courage to single-handedly kill a stag in its sexual prime. Once this had been achieved, he would take on the sexual essence of the stag and in that guise would return home to mate with the Earth Mother on sacred ceremonial sites. Their union symbolised the continuation of the tribe, as well as acting as a blessing for the land and the spirit of the animal which has sacrificed its life for the benefit of the community. Thus a woman's magic and her sexuality was an accepted part of the natural lores of nature.

## Meeting the priestess

### SETTING UP

This ritual is more suited to the privacy of home. You are preparing to meet a very powerful ancient element of yourself, so I recommend you create some sort of temple as part of your preparation work. This could be making a simple altar by lighting candles and incense or by drawing your own vision of what your temple looks like. By doing this you may find that certain symbols spring to mind or you may be drawn to particular animal totems. Animals have always played an important role in the life of priestesses. You may also feel that you become attracted to certain colours and fabrics or want to dress in a particular way. What headdress would you wear, and what type of climate would you live in if you were this priestess? Are you drawn to a special power symbol such as a staff or do you wish to wear a particular mystical symbol? Remember, this is your own personal adventure and therefore very much open to your own interpretation. It may also be fun to do this with friends, so you can share your visions and insights.

### PREPARING YOURSELF

Make sure you are comfortable. Light your candles and incense, and take some deep breaths to relax. It may feel appropriate to stand up or walk around at some stage. Just go with what comes to you and enjoy it because you are giving yourself the opportunity of experiencing the magnificence of being a representative of the Goddess on earth.

When you feel ready, close your eyes and call on your priestess to present her power symbolically to you. She might be a snake priestess as in my case, or a moon priestess, or some goddess archetype such as Athena, Diana, Hecate, etc. (See pages 137–148.) By embracing your divine priestess you now have the opportunity to make a vow of commitment that you will bear witness to the light; to set a living example of love, grace and gratitude; to be an embodiment for the Goddess to express her energy of compassion, beauty and wisdom. This is not a vow to be made lightly. It also means that you are prepared to take full responsibility for your sexual expression; that every time you enter into a sexual union, you are enacting the mystical marriage of *hieros gamos*. It is immaterial whether this means swinging from the chandeliers, dressing up in leather, chains and feather boa, or gazing deeply into your partner's eyes. What matters is that you are conscious of carrying the energy of the divine feminine in her ultimate expression.

Allow yourself to explore what it feels like to be a woman who is proud of her sexuality and how this can serve the Goddess. Notice any negative thoughts or opinions which may have stopped you from becoming a magical woman in her full glory. Ask your priestess to help you release them. Breathe them out of your body. By doing this you are beginning a fantastic sexual healing process which will allow you to become a far more integrated woman in your daily life. When you feel ready, write down what you have learnt about yourself and make a list of any negative patterns which prevent you from living the type of life that you wish for. Put this on your temple altar and leave it there until you feel that you have resolved these things. Allow the candles to burn down in their entirety and gives thanks to your priestess by leaving an appropriate offering on the altar for her. At some point, this can be taken into nature and buried at the base of a tree.

## BRINGING THE PRIESTESS INTO LIFE

No matter what your sexual preference is, normally as you become more respectful of yourself as a woman, you will automatically want to create meaningful and satisfying sexual relationships. I know a woman who now calls upon her priestess in her mind's eye to grant a blessing on the union between herself and her partner every time they make love. It has made an enormous difference in the way they treat each other both in and out of bed, even though her partner has no idea about what she is doing! That is the beauty of woman's magic at work. When you work consciously with your priestess you will find yourself standing taller in every way and this, of course, adds to the mystique of who you are.

# The Prostitute

With the destruction and desecration of the sacred role of the priestess, woman's sexuality has fallen from grace. Without the divine connection with the Goddess, we as women lose sight of who we truly are – and sadly our sexuality becomes enveloped in shallow relationships, abusive behaviour and unworthy conduct. Thus the archetypal prostitute resides in all of us.

The prostitute is the part of us that sells our souls short for material gain or social status. It is the fortune-seeking Mata Hari in us which desperately wants that part in a film, to further our careers, to enter high social circles, to marry 'well', to cast enchantment for our own ends. Think of the beautiful young girl, sporting diamonds and fur coat, and upon her arm staggers the provider of her trinkets, an old, creaking millionaire. There is also another kind of prostitution which is much more insidious and unconscious. These are the women who sacrifice their sense of self in deference to their husbands' careers and children's welfare. By the time their children have flown the nest, they are left in a void, not knowing who they are, and the relationship with their husband has dwindled into polite pleasantries. They unwillingly settle for it for fear of the unknown and spend the rest of their lives living a role as wife and mother, but never as who they really are. Then, finally, there are our sisters who do indeed sell their bodies for money on street corners and in seedy hotels as well as those who serve politically influential circles. This is a dark world where women, more often than not, become victims of abuse, betrayal and violence. Yet some do willingly provide a very valuable and much needed service.

By acknowledging your own prostitute within, you can come to terms with your own code of ethics; what is morally acceptable to you. And remember this is personal; some women are completely comfortable with their decision to better themselves through the use of their bodies.

 ## Embracing the prostitute

### SETTING UP
This may be the first time that you have ever considered this part of yourself, so to help forge a link with your inner prostitute, I suggest that you set up some sort of shrine to

her. This could be done by creating a montage of pictures and headlines which describe all her different facets. Alternatively you may want to collect certain symbols or articles of clothing which feed her. It also may be appropriate to play loud, raunchy striptease music to get into her character. Let your imagination take control, and enjoy it! With humour you can move mountains.

## PREPARING YOURSELF

Allow yourself to become relaxed and, when you feel ready, close your eyes and call to your prostitute. Really explore her image in full. She may be shockingly wanton, or in desperate need of comfort. She may be sly, manipulative and cunning, or angry and vengeful. Just remember she is a very powerful part of your psyche and therefore deeply influential in the way you behave subconsciously, especially in relationships with men. She also holds the key to your sexual healing. Until we face our sexual shame we are trapped in self-doubt, guilt and remorse. Facing your prostitute will help you to understand your negative behaviour patterns, and will provide you with the chance to come to terms with them. Once this has been achieved, you will feel much freer in who you are and how you express yourself.

## HONOURING YOUR PAST

You can perform a candle-lighting ritual as part of self-forgiveness each time you need to come to terms with past sexual behaviour which you realise was abusive, manipulative or untruthful. By releasing yourself from these shames, you also release those people who suffered through your actions. These rituals will have a profound effect on the way your life and relationships develop in the future.

It is also a powerful gesture to light candles for the millions of women, children and men who are prostitutes around the world. Too many are forced into this through extortion and have no choice whatsoever. If appropriate, give thanks that this is not your personal destiny, by the grace of God.

# The Evil Temptress or the Wise Witch Woman

In Christian traditions, the only permissible religious persona of a woman was that of Mary, an untouched virgin, even though she had 'entertained' a representative from the higher realms, much like the temple priestesses. (It is interesting to note that the word *virgin* originally meant unmarried rather than untainted.)

With the rise of the Christian church across Europe all the ancient fertility rituals and associated beliefs were forced underground. As the power of the church increased, it started to mock those who continued to celebrate in the old ways. Suddenly the Goddess was regarded as an evil enchantress and the Horned God as the devil himself. Women particularly suffered from persecution because they inherently followed the natural rhythms of the earth and moon cycles; they enabled creation to take place; they held the power to carry life within their bodies; and only they knew the true identities of the fathers of their babies. Far worse than that, a woman was the temptress or evil witch (Eve) who wove unholy thoughts in the soul of pious man (Adam). The infamous *Malleus Maleficarum* (Hammer of Witches), written by two Dominican monks, specified that women were generally more inclined towards witchcraft because 'all witchcraft comes from carnal lust, which in women is insatiable'. (Who exactly is projecting what on to whom, I wonder!) Woman therefore held the key to their physical and spiritual destruction. In fact, to stamp out any affiliation with the ancient fertility rituals and particularly with the Goddess, the joy of sex was deemed to be a sin by the church and any sexual activity outside marriage was completely banned. Procreation within marriage was its only acceptable motivation, and any form of contraception was considered to be as sinful as murder. The church also cast a ban on the number of days a married couple could procreate. Sex was made illegal on Fridays, Sundays and Wednesdays. It was also illegal for forty days before Christmas and Easter, and for three days before taking communion!

## Paying homage to the wise witch

Our 'evil temptress' is in fact our wise witch. She is our lineage guardian for all the injustice we have suffered at the hands of our men, just for being women. It is she who stands in defiance – willing to be burnt at the stake for what she believes. It is she who kept the old ways and lores alive, who secretly met with other brave souls to celebrate the old crafts out of love for the Earth Goddess. Your evil temptress or wise witch is that force of truth that will not lie down and die. She will make you listen to your heart and give you the courage to fight for what you believe against great adversity. She also gives you comfort when you feel isolated because you have rocked the boat through following your heart.

### SETTING UP

This ritual can be conducted outside in nature or at home, depending on your own preference. Since this is honouring the part of yourself which has suffered from age-old persecution, you may want to share it with other female friends who feel equally in need of honouring this facet of themselves.

This ritual is perfect as a fire ceremony. Build a bonfire or hearth fire and use it to burn out the old and welcome in the new. The fire also acts as a symbolic remembrance to all those women who died in the flames because of the injustice, paranoia and prejudice of their times.

## PREPARING YOURSELF

Close your eyes and relax. Call on your wise witch to make herself known to you. Ask for her blessing and then invite her to show you scenes from your past where you stopped yourself from expressing who you really are. People and situations may come to mind, so write them down. Once you have done this, relive the situation in your mind's eye and clearly see that even though you may have felt threatened and undermined, the source of your power was, and is, ever present. Witness yourself taking back control of the situation by speaking your truth as the extraordinary and awesome woman that you are. Show yourself to your persecutor in your full magnificence and see their control over you disintegrate and diminish to nothing. Beside their names, write a short note of forgiveness, and when you feel complete, throw your list in the fire. Feel it burn out all your anger, resentment and hatred. If you are with friends, share your experiences with each other, and then join hands to remember those women around the world who are still suffering from persecution just for being women. Ritual work such as this is vital and powerful: every living soul will be affected in some way. It is also a wonderful opportunity to make a personal vow that you are willing to become a witness to truth no matter what the world may throw in your path. This is a great challenge for us all, and one that needs support from friends who are also as committed to the truth.

# Woman's Magic in Sexuality

## CALLING FOR HELP

It is particularly beneficial to work with your wise witch when you are facing some sort of sexual discrimination or when suffering from sexual harassment. By linking with her, you can find the wisdom to deal with it in an appropriate way. It may be that you will have to seek help from others or you may find you can change the energy of the situation through powerful inner communication with her. Forming a relationship with your wise witch is not about promoting feminism, rather it is concerned with finding the source of power and justice that you inherently have, and deeply believe in. It is also about educating others to face their own discriminatory shortcomings whether they want to or not.

I want to conclude this with an extraordinary poem which was given to me by a male friend who is a devoted follower of the Goddess and the old ways. It says it all:

For all those who died – stripped naked, shaved, shorn
For all those who screamed in vain to the Great Goddess, only to
have their tongues ripped out by the root,
For all those who were pricked, racked, broken on the wheel for
the sins of their Inquisitors
For all those whose beauty stirred their torturers to fury;
and for those whose ugliness did the same.
For all those who were neither ugly nor beautiful, but only
women who would not submit.
For all those whose quick fingers, broken in the vice.
For all those soft arms, pulled from their sockets.
For all those budding breasts, ripped with hot pincers,
For all those midwives, killed merely for the sin of delivering
man to an imperfect world.

For all those witch-women, my sisters who breathed freer as the
flames took them, knowing as they shed their female bodies,
the seared flesh falling like fruit in the flames,
that death alone would cleanse them of the sin for which they
died – the sin of being born a woman who is more than
the sum of her parts.

*Anonymous, 16th century*
(Published in E. Jong, *Witches*, New York 1981.)

# The Triple Face of the Moon

In Greek mythology, the moon was thought to represent the three
sexual phases of woman: the new moon as Persephone, Goddess of
the Underworld, the virgin; the full moon as Demeter, Goddess
of the Earth, the mother; and the dark moon as Hecate, Goddess
of Witchcraft and Enchantment, the hag or crone of death and
destruction. These three phases are also enacted with the female
body every month and this also affects our emotional make-up. In
Native American traditions, and among many other indigenous
tribes, women refer to their menstruation as their 'moon time'.
Their men realised that a woman's psychic ability increased during
her bleeding time, and respectfully allowed her to enjoy a private
space in which to explore this mystical part of herself. Women
withdraw from the main camp into their own 'moon lodge' where
they take part in sacred cleansing rituals which open up their
psychic centres. Through meditation, chanting and prayer they are
able to gain extraordinary insights into the future of the tribe and,
therefore, give guidance to the elders as they re-emerge.

This custom could be usefully revived in our own culture. I
believe that most women suffer from pre-menstrual tension
because we are under so much pressure to hold our lives and
families together, there is no room to consider the natural flow of
our psychic energies. This can lead to depression and violent

mood swings because it is nature's way of showing that a woman inherently needs time to herself during her menstruation because it realigns her energies with those of the moon. This connection is the very essence of femininity.

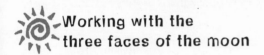

## Working with the three faces of the moon

### SETTING UP

Since the moon is the guardian of woman's magic as well as her sexuality, it is important to pay homage to her on a regular monthly basis, just as our ancestors did. These monthly meetings traditionally take place on the full moon and are known as *esbats*. Women gather together to set objectives, share experiences and make merry. However the phases of the moon are also important if you want to manifest something in your life.

### PREPARING YOURSELF

To manifest something in your life, set up an altar or sacred space during the new moon phase where you can light candles, and keep special objects or pictures which empower your dreams and aspirations. Ask Persephone, the face of waiting potential, to bless it. As the moon moves into its full phase, ask for the power of Demeter, the face of fulfillment, to bring it into being. **Then let it go.** By trusting in the process and rhythm of the universal flow, your desire will come to you in exactly the way that is best for your highest growth, and at precisely the right moment.

Should you wish to release unwanted emotional baggage, or say goodbye to something like an old relationship, conduct your ritual during the waning phase of the moon which takes on the face of Hecate, the

17

destroyer. Do remember, however, that there is a universal law which stipulates that when you point the finger of blame, or actively wish someone harm, it will reverberate upon the creator of that intent with ten times as much force. So respect other people's paths and destinies, and just work on yourself.

 ## Meeting the Triple Goddess

### SETTING UP

Meeting with your archetypes of the Triple Goddess takes you on a journey of a lifetime – you can see yourself in the future through the eyes of your crone. After all it is she you are becoming. If you don't like what you see, then you know you have to make changes in your life.

It is very powerful to conduct this ritual over the full moon, although it is perfectly acceptable to follow your own timing as well. Create an altar and place four white candles on it. Decorate it with flowers, crystals and perhaps images and pictures which symbolise the three faces of the Goddess.

### PREPARING YOURSELF

Light the first candle, then close your eyes and ask the vision of Persephone to appear to you. Notice every detail about her. Ask her for a gift for your highest learning. This may come as a vision, a feeling or an inspiration. Allow whatever comes into your mind's eye just to be as it is. Once you feel complete with her, give thanks to her. Open your eyes, light the second candle and invite Demeter to step forward. Again, ask her for a gift for your highest learning and see what comes into your mind's eye. Once you feel complete, give thanks to her. Light the third candle, and now invite Hecate to come forward. Ask for your gift and acknowledge it. Now invite the three goddesses to stand side by side and see what their relationship is like. It is important to notice if the three archetypes are in harmony, or if there is conflict between them. Should conflict be in evidence, you have an important key to work with. When conflict resides within your psyche, it causes havoc in your reality. Ask each one what changes you need to make in your life for harmony to be restored, and notice any physical sensations in your body. Be aware that you are performing a powerful inner healing as you harmonise with your Triple Goddess.

Once you are complete, light the fourth candle in celebration of the Triple Goddess and allow all four candles to burn down in their entirety. Write down what you have experienced, and keep a record of your dreams. You may well find that prophetic messages, answers to problems or creative inspiration whispers in your ear during the night or as you wake up in the morning.

By paying homage to the Triple Goddess you are psychically linking with the mystical energies of the moon. This feeds your inner woman, and helps you to embrace all the different facets of yourself. By doing so, it will enable you to reveal the goddess that you really are.

# Chapter 2
# Woman's Magic
## at Home

**S**INCE THE HOME LIES UNDER the domain of the moon, this is where the heart of a woman's magic naturally resides. Our home is also an outer expression of who we are inside. So a harmonious relationship with it is paramount for a successful, contented and, of course, a magical life.

The principles of feng shui are beginning to cleave deeply into the most cynical of households – people from all walks of life are searching for ways to create better relationships and for more success to come in their working lives. I am all for this, yet although I too adhere to some basic feng shui rules, at the end of the day I get very confused by what does what to what because this is an enigmatic Eastern concept trying to fit into a Western linear mind. Too much of this or that, and it would appear that your entire life is in danger of being thrown into chaos! I incorporate the laws of Celtic magic to harmonise my home because this is the wisdom of my heritage and it feels as if it has been ground into my bones.

## Merging with the Magic

I believe that every home is alive with its own magic, and once you begin to merge with this magic, your home will start to work with you in all sorts of extraordinary ways. It is as if it becomes an extension of you, and an intimate communication starts to occur. Several years ago, this happened to a friend who suddenly became obsessed with making her bedroom more feminine. She had been divorced for years and although she had been out on dates, she had never gelled with anyone in particular. Out of the blue she suddenly felt the urge to buy a rose-covered duvet cover and pillowcases. This surprised her because rosecovered anything was certainly not her style. However, she became even more confused when she felt the impulse to spray her new bed linen with a mixture of jasmine and rose oils. She also felt a need to change the position of her bed, and to completely clear out all the clutter. She then invested money in new curtains which were covered with stars. She began to make other changes in the house too. Everything had to be 'just so'. As the days rolled by, an inner knowing grew stronger and stronger that she was going to meet someone special. Lo and behold, she received an invitation to an impromptu party. As she was getting ready something told her that this was the night that she would meet this person. She did indeed! As she walked up to greet her host, he literally handed her into the arms of her future lover! It was as if her home somehow told her to prepare for her new boyfriend.

The magic also happens when you buy a home. I am always very conscious of how I feel about a place the moment I walk into it. I either feel comfortable and 'welcomed' – it is a wonderful experience to enter into a place which is well loved and therefore loves well – or I can't wait to escape. Some places feel so repellent and possessed by unhappy ghosts they can give you the goose bumps – and it requires another form of magic called exorcism to release them.

In ancient times, it was normal practice to pay homage to the custodial devic entity which guarded your hearth and I am sure it is this entity which creates the ambience or feeling of a place. I have also always believed that it is the house which buys us, rather than us buying it. If you don't fit, you don't stand a chance of moving in. Perhaps it does depend on whether the custodial deva takes a shine to you or not! My friend Lou is convinced her present house chose her. Before she even knew the house existed, she bought two large salmon pink sofas with matching cushions which did little for the house she was living in. However, a few months later she went to look at her present house, and knew instantly this was the one for her because this is where her sofas were obviously meant to live. Their colour matched the décor and style of the house perfectly. Ever since she moved in, her life has taken dramatic turns for the better. Another friend, Sarah, dreamed about her future home several years ago. She knew it was somewhere quite isolated, but had land and outbuildings attached. Sure enough, as the years passed by, her desire for an old farmhouse with land propelled her to search in the outer reaches of Somerset. As she went to view one particular property and found herself round the back of it, she instantly recognised it from her dream. The house exchange went effortlessly, and she is now restoring it to its former glory. She knows this is where she is to spend the rest of her life.

So how do you feel when you cross your threshold? Just take a few moments to visualise the effect that this has upon you. Do you close the door against the world and breathe a sigh of relief, or do you feel as if you have entered a prison, a war zone or a rubbish tip? If it's a negative response, then it's time to make changes. Sometimes this can be as radical as moving house, but more often a lick of paint, a clear out, and a cleansing ritual will start the ball rolling.

## Looking at Your Home with Open Eyes!

Before we get into the nitty-gritty of making merry magic, now is the perfect opportunity to take a good long look at your home environment to get a better understanding of how you tick on a subconscious level. For instance, if it is full of paraphernalia billowing out of corners and cupboards, it indicates that you are probably a poor timekeeper and one of those who takes hours just to find a pair of shoes. Decision-making won't be too hot either and it is well known that those who live in confusion and chaos suffer from chronic tiredness. Hoarding also indicates an inability to let go of the past, so hoarders seldom create their dreams.

However, should your home be so clinically clean that you can't bear a thing out of place, it indicates that you want to be rigidly in control of anything and everyone that comes your way. It may be that you tend to be critical and unyielding to other people's ideas as well as indicating a dislike for sex! Perhaps this is the origin of the wonderful proverb: 'boring women have immaculate homes' – but that's no excuse to swing too far the other way! A woman who is comfortable with her magic allows a flow into her home which gives space for things to breathe and to evolve in a natural way. In fact her home often gives the impression that it is a physical extension of those mystical realms; a home where magic oozes from every nook and cranny, and something wonderful could happen at any moment.

Finding and moving into a house is said to be the second most stressful thing we can do to ourselves; the first being a break-up of a relationship. However with the use of ritual, we can smooth the path to locate a perfect nest. Being the proverbial rolling stone, I have moved many times but I have ceased to worry about finding a suitable place to live. With a little help from the old crafts, my ancestors, guides and angels, I focus on what I want and it never fails to manifest exactly when and where I need it. This is exactly what I did to find my present home.

# Manifesting a Place to Live

It had been a long-time ambition of mine to move to the south coast, to a particular area which is very sought after. I wanted the archetypal cottage in the country. Everyone, on hearing this, sucked their teeth and said I would never be able to find anywhere to rent without paying over the odds. This kind of attitude is like a red rag to a bull for me. So I wrote down a list of everything I wanted in a home to make me feel comfortable. Since I am a writer I need peace and quiet, and the inspiration of being in a rural setting, yet I also wanted to be near a town which had good social and sporting amenities. I wanted two bedrooms, one of which could double up as a study-cum-spare room, and an open fireplace in the sitting room so I could toast my toes in the winter. Past the age of shivering in unheated houses, I asked for central heating, and a garden which wasn't too demanding. I had plenty of my own furniture so it needed to be unfurnished, but I lacked a cooker and a wardrobe. I also asked for quiet, yet helpful and friendly neighbours. I lit a candle, and asked for the universe to grant me this wish. I gave thanks and made an offering to the Goddess which I buried underneath a tree. I then put my list away and got on with my life. Shortly after that, I was offered a part-time job in the area in which I wanted to live. Synchronistically, my boss asked me if I wanted a cottage which had just come up for rent on his land. The location was perfect, the rent affordable and it had everything I asked for on my list down to the cooker and wardrobe being in-situ! And I never had to step foot inside an estate agency or look in the property list of local newspapers.

When you want to move, make a list of exactly how you want your new home to be. Light a candle and ask the universe, or whatever godhead you believe in, to grant you this wish. You can also empower this wish by doing your ritual just before the full moon because of the moon's association with the home. Then forget about it and trust that it will be provided for you. Before the cottage manifested, I used to have fun thinking what this new place was going to be like, but I was totally unattached to how it was going to come about – because I knew it would. When you have implicit trust that the power of the universal force works in tandem with your own innate power, your home and anything else for that matter, will manifest. Just listen to your intuition or that gut feeling, and you will be led right to its door.

## Moving In

As soon as you have taken possession of your new *dulce domum*, it is very wise to do what is known as a space-clearing ritual. This clears the decks of any unwanted negative energies and breaks the ties with the previous owners or tenants, while enabling you to put your own enigmatic stamp on to it. Performing rituals like this right from the start produces a magical atmosphere packed with love, reverence, warmth and welcome which will automatically benefit anyone who visits. This really needs to be done before any decoration takes place. Even though decorating is a very effective space-clearer in its own right, the use of ritual symbolises that you are consciously entering into the magical flow of the home itself. This also establishes a sense of protection and safety which is important for peace of mind. In addition, I believe it is significant to realise that although money may have exchanged hands, and there could be a large mortgage involved, you are in reality only a custodian to this haven for as long as destiny decides. Houses have a much longer life span than mere mortals and it's our responsibility as custodians to make sure it glows with as much love as we can give it until we hand it on.

The name of a house is also important because of the interpretation it carries and how it energetically influences what happens to the house. For example, a friend rented a gorgeous fourteenth-century cottage which had been renamed after a much-loved dog by its previous owner. The dog was buried, plaque and all, under a beautiful flowering cherry tree in the centre of the garden. Yet after this had happened, the fortunes of the cottage abruptly changed. The elderly owner could no longer look after the cottage so she gave it to a national organisation. Very soon it became a rental cottage which is how my friend came to live there. Although it was later bought by a private owner it still continued as a rental cottage. It is as if the cottage belongs to the dog, and no human is destined to settle there until the name is changed. So if you have inherited a house name, make sure it sits well with you, and provides the right type of vibe that you want the house to carry. If it doesn't, don't be afraid to change it, but make sure you ritualistically burn or bury the old name to make way for your own new one. You can incorporate this into the following 'moving in' space-clearing ritual.

 ## Space-clearing ritual

The most auspicious time to do a cleansing ritual is during the build-up to the full moon. This means that you will be evoking the moon's blessings which are full of potential and fruitfulness. All those who are to be part of the household need to gather together with a bowl of salt water. Salt has been used as a purifier for centuries; in fact Christians used to use it in their churches and homes to ward off evil.

First, you need to walk or stamp out the entire outer borders of your new property, sprinkling the salted water as you go, and banishing any negative influences which may be lurking. (If your new home is in a block of flats, then walk the interior boundary of your apartment.) Some people bang gongs, dance, and have a good yell. Sound dissipates all sorts of things, so go on and have some fun with it. OK, your neighbours may be a bit flummoxed – send them good thoughts too, and make it up to them later! (Talking of neighbours, if you are one of those to suffer with neighbours from hell, this ritual will certainly move energy between you both, and don't be surprised if things are resolved in the most unusual way. Just be willing for everything to turn out best for everyone concerned.)

You now need to do this in every room in the house, paying particular attention to the corners where energy tends to become trapped and, of course, the cellars and attics. If there is any part of the house you don't feel comfortable about, leave a bowl of salted water in the centre of the floor overnight with a burning incense stick. You can also rebalance the energy of the room by simply placing two open sea-shells on the floor in opposing diagonal corners. I have no idea why this works, but for some reason it does.

It is now time to decorate to your own taste. If this is not necessary, at least wash down all the walls and ceilings with salted water, and make sure the carpets are well and truly cleaned. And don't leave any room out just because it's not going to be used that much. It would be like missing out on washing one of your fingers or toes. Once the decoration has been completed, it is time to perform a house-blessing ceremony to which you can invite all your friends to help you celebrate, and to make your home a truly joyful place to be.

 ## House-blessing ceremony

Your kids will love to do this too. The young are much more receptive to the natural flow of magic anyway, and will probably provide all sorts of incredible insights to the proceedings.

Make a small bonfire in a favourite spot in the garden, or light a fire inside in the hearth, or if neither are appropriate, light two silver candles and some incense. Create a ring with all the people present, shut your eyes and allow yourself to relax. Enter into the mystical flow of the house, and start to feel its energy. Feel as if you are becoming part of it as it is part of you. If you like, you can call on its devic custodian to appear in your mind's eye. See what it's like, how old it is, and what kind of personality it has. Greet it and ask for blessings of harmony and grace to exist between you. You can also invite the devic custodian to give you a symbolic gift which can come as a thought, image or feeling. The entity may also wish to pass on information to you which may benefit both you and the house in some way. Just accept what happens, and allow yourself to enjoy the encounter.

If you feel this is too way out, or that your guests may be a little overwhelmed by meeting devic entities, then ask the Goddess, your own deity, or the universal force to bring blessings of harmony and happiness to your home. You can do this by lighting a special 'smudge stick' which has been made from sage. (You can quite easily make your own by growing sage and drying it.) This is the traditional method Native American Indians have used for centuries to cleanse, purify and bless their lodges, and is now becoming increasingly popular here too. Once the smudge stick is alight, blow out the flame so it is smoking. Make sure you have a heatproof dish to catch the ashes, and begin to spread the smoke throughout the room while calling on the blessings of the Goddess. It is also a wonderful gesture to incorporate the four directions of north, south, east and west, as well as their devic entities.

This symbolises the flow of nature being incorporated into your own home.

First, turn to the east, the place where the sylphs of air reside, and ask them to grant your home with clear thinking and illumination. Now turn to the south and invite the blessings of the salamanders of the fiery realms to manifest as inspiration, passion for life and love, and adaptability in the face of change. Next, turn to the west to welcome the undines from the water realms to grant emotional stability and balance, and to create a home where your inner visions and dreams can manifest. Finally, turn to the north, and ask the gnomes of the earth to bring abundance, fertility and prosperity into your home. Give thanks to these wonderful magical realms and now, together with your guests, start to smudge all the rooms in your home, asking for blessings and giving thanks as you go. Your guests can bang drums, or play pipes, or just enter into the fun of it all by dancing round! I also pay special attention to my front door, and ask for blessings to come to anyone who enters through it. You can make up your own ritual which is comfortable for you. Once you are complete, put the smudge stick out in some sand or with a sprinkle of water, and then gather your guests together in a circle by linking hands, and spend a few moments quietly listening to the sound of your wonderful magical home.

Always end any ritual ceremony by giving thanks for what you have, and by offering something into the fire as a symbolic gesture of gratitude, like some incense, or perhaps a special twig, nut or piece of fruit. Your guests may want to do this too. And now it's time for that house-warming party! This traditionally needs to include offerings of food and drink brought as a hearth warmer by your guests.

The gesture symbolises blessings for fertility, fruitfulness and joy to come to your home.

# Using Ritual as an Ongoing Blessing

You can use this kind of space-clearing ritual at any time you feel the need, whether alone or with others. This also includes the aftermath of visiting relatives, a hearty row with a partner, or even when the children are sending you mad. I regularly throw open the windows and play a blast of music to dissipate negativity when there's been bad feeling, or when I am particularly irritated by someone or something. I don't want that to be carried by my home any longer than needs be. I also always do a space-clearing ritual with a smudge stick after any visitors depart to make sure they don't leave anything of themselves behind. While doing it, I send them loving and grateful thoughts for being in my life, wish them a safe journey home, and then make sure that the harmony of the house is restored.

After I have had a cleaning blitz I smudge all the rooms and doorways as well, which clears any dust in the ethers and lifts the mood of the house. I find it especially helpful when cabin fever threatens. This is a syndrome which those who work from home will know well!

# When the Walls Close In

Cleansing rituals are also useful whenever you feel low. We all suffer from the lows because without them we can't have the highs, but it is in the privacy of our own homes that the walls may feel as if they are literally coming in on us. Many people are now visiting their doctors' surgeries suffering from some sort of debilitating depression including chronic tiredness. I believe that most of our depressions are caused by feelings of loneliness and isolation. If I ever feel the clouds beginning to gather, I always do a ritual to honour the process. This is because I have learnt over the years that when I enter into a bleak time, something miraculous is about to manifest for my greatest good providing I let it – and this means working through the darkness. This has never failed to give me the strength and courage to trust that everything is evolving in my life just as it is meant to be, and I am always deeply grateful to have a home where I feel safe and secure while I wait for the darkness to pass. This is the ritual I use to help it on its way.

 ### Ritual for releasing depression

Create a quiet space for yourself, and light two silver candles to represent the moon and self-illumination, as well as woman's magic. By doing this act alone, you will feel more connected with your higher self. Take some paper and coloured pens, and either draw your feelings or write about them. Keep drawing or writing until you completely run out of steam. You often find that messages from deep in your subconscious may surface which give you a clue as to why you are feeling as you are. It could be age-old rage with someone, or self-hatred, or because you have completely lost touch with your life's purpose. Perhaps your body is telling you to completely change your diet. Just let it be what it is. Now, light a gold or yellow candle (gold and yellow represent inspiration and clarity, as well as affirming that sunny days will return), together with some of your favourite incense, perhaps put on some soothing music, and take time to consider what you have created. You also need to allow yourself really to feel this depression, to enter into the blackness and speak with it. To do this, I always ask for the protection of the loving light of my higher self. I then ask for my darkness to appear as an archetypal animal in my mind's eye. It can appear as a terrifying monster which needs to be released from a cage. I confront it by asking what message it has for me, and after I receive this message, I imagine a door opening in my psyche and watch the monster drop out, wishing it well as it goes. Sometimes it's a half-starved creature which just needs love, so I work with that. See what comes to you, and just trust that your psyche is both potent and powerful as a self-healing tool. It is important, however, that when you meet with your archetypal animal, you work with it. Find out what message it has for you, and then release it in some way. By doing this you begin to release yourself from the root cause of your depression. You have to let the darkness out of your psyche for the light to rekindle itself again. For some people, inner visioning can be difficult to achieve, so draw or write about it instead. Let your imagination take you to the truth. You possess the key to self-knowledge, and it is this self-knowledge which will put you back on the path again.

Once you have completed this exercise, ceremonially burn your papers in the flame of the gold or yellow candle, or you can put them into a hearth fire. Give thanks to the moon for its wisdom, and to the sun for its power and everlasting glorious light. Allow the candles to burn down in their entirety, so make sure they are in a safe place. You can finish off this ritual by treating yourself to a luxurious candlelit bath with lots of bubbles, a handful of salt (which will cleanse your body and psyche) and some wonderful essential oils such as lavender, rosemary and sandalwood. And keep praying for the light to enter back into your soul. I assure you it will.

# Confronting Loneliness

To conclude, I would like to tell you about an insight I gleaned about loneliness which really made me sit up and take notice. As I have already said, I believe most of our depressive problems are caused by feelings of loneliness and isolation. Yet, although I learnt long ago that my expectations of happiness could never be fulfilled by another person, it still didn't stop feelings of isolation when they hit. In fact it made the whole thing worse because I felt that as a spiritually aware person I should be beyond it all. One day when I was feeling particularly alone, suffering from cabin fever, and at a loss to know how to deal with it, I went for a walk around an ancient sacred site, and I asked the custodial ancestors of the site to help me understand what loneliness was really about. My question was answered thus:

> Loneliness happens when we are disconnected from our
> own special purpose in life. Depression is the symptom
> which manifests to make us take notice that we need to
> start searching for it; it happens when we are disconnected
> from our own spiritual centre, the source of our creativity
> and the love of what we do in the service of others.

In that moment, I suddenly realised that was my problem. I wasn't doing what I loved to do. In fact I was sitting around doing nothing – and I hate doing nothing! Hence my entire being was yelling at me to start working at something I loved again. As soon as I became creatively motivated, the loneliness vanished in a twinkle of an eye. This is also why another person, or even partner, may help us find our path, but they can't live it for us. We have to do it for ourselves because this is what we came to this earth to do, and anyway they have their own personal creative destiny to sort out. Several days later I was pondering upon the truth of what I had gleaned, and became drawn to Marianne Williamson's book, *A Return to Love*. I opened it at random, and this by pure magical synchronicity is what the first paragraph said:

> Success means we go to sleep at night knowing that our talents and abilities were used in a way that served others. We're compensated by grateful looks in people's eyes, whatever material abundance supports us in performing joyfully and at high energy, and the magnificent feeling that we did our bit today to save the world.
>
> The atonement means putting love first. In everything. In business as well as everything else. You're in business to spread love. Your screenplay should spread love. Your hair salon should spread love. Your agency should spread love. Your life should spread love. The key to a successful career is realising that it's not separate from the rest of your life, but is rather an extension of your most basic self. And your most basic self is love!

This means that our homes should spread love too.

## The Core of a Woman's Magic

Doing what you love to do, loving what you do, and feeling safe where you live is the core of a woman's magic. So, if you feel as though your life is completely worthless, you now have an important key. And if you hate what you do in your working life, or you feel that you are living in the wrong place – it's time to make some changes.

 **Ritual for finding your life's purpose**
Create a quiet, harmonious ambience at home by lighting some candles and incense. Close your eyes, and invite your

spirit guide to manifest in your mind's eye. Ask your guide to give you a gift which will symbolise where your destiny lies. Watch or feel your guide pull out the gift from deep inside your heart. Again, this could come as a feeling, as a thought, or as a vision. If you don't get anything, don't worry. By making this connection with your higher self, and acknowledging that this is what you dearly desire to come to you, the ball will start rolling one way or another. Once you feel complete, give thanks to your guide and your higher wisdom, and open your eyes. Write down what you have discovered and allow the candles to burn down in their entirety. You may need to form a long-term plan to manifest your life's purpose from where you stand at present, or you may be able to start making changes immediately. To help you stay centred and focused, create a special corner or space somewhere at home, or at your workplace, where you can put an image, picture, relevant symbol or an inspirational piece of writing which will continually remind you of where you are heading. For example, to help me stay focused on my own life's purpose I keep a framed Wayne Dwyer quote by my computer: 'I choose to be a host for God's love; not a hostage to my ego.' You can also update your corner as more realisations materialise. As your path begins to unfold, add to your space all the names of people and synchronistic circumstances which have helped you to find it, and begin to get into the habit of practising gratitude.

## Practising Gratitude

Learning how to be grateful for what we have and what we receive is a vital part of woman's magic because gratitude spreads love and, as far as I'm concerned, learning to love is the reason we are all here. It's all too easy to forget how lucky we are, especially as life becomes more frenetic and pressurised. To help with this, I created a magical tree of gratitude which reminds me to count my blessings no matter what is happening around me.

## Making a magical tree of gratitude

It is simple to create your own magical tree. All you need is to find a small branch fallen from a favourite tree, or buy a long, twisted willow branch from your local florist. Plant your branch firmly into a terracotta pot, filled with soil, which you could decorate with your own symbols for abundance, love and blessings, and place it somewhere in the house which feels appropriate to you. Mine is by my front door so every time I leave and return, there it is as a fond farewell and a warm welcome. You can also cover the top of the soil with stones. I've used hag stones. Hag stones have natural holes made in them by the elements which, in the old days, were considered to be very auspicious since they represented the fertility of the Mother Goddess. These can be found on pebble beaches around the south coast.

Next, make a sign for your tree of gratitude which you hang on one of its branches which gives thanks to the spirit of the tree itself and for its magical qualities. For example, the magical properties of willow are wisdom, love and protection; willow is also associated with enchantment and moon magic. Oak represents strength and ancient knowledge; beech grants wishes; maple attracts love. (For more on this see Chapter 3, Women's Magic in the Garden.) Then, as a blessing comes to you in the form of a new friend, a precious gift, a significant change of direction, a new love or an important life lesson learnt, make a beautiful label of gratitude and hang it on your tree.

As the year progresses, so your tree will be filled with your appreciation. The more you say thank you, the more the universe provides you with things to be thankful for.

At the end of the year you can either keep your labels as a reminder of what has happened for you, or create a thanksgiving ritual where you burn them in a fire as a gesture of gratitude to the Goddess. Each year you can choose a different tree or use the same one, it is up to you. Everyone who comes to my home loves my tree, and I am often given special things to put on it. I also put any letters or cards I receive which thank me in some way at its base because this symbolises the universal cycle of giving and receiving.

It's a great way to get children involved with learning gratitude too; each could have their own tree to look after. You could also introduce the concept at work because this can be a hotbed of negativity, and it's small gestures like this which can make a huge difference. At the end of the day most people love to feel appreciated and want to give appreciation because – surprise, surprise – it makes them feel good. So I wish your magical tree to overflow with gratitude and blessings.

You can use gratitude to help sell your home as well.

Selling a house can be equally as stressful as buying one, especially when you become part of a chain, a bridging loan is staring you in the face, or you can't start a new life until you've left the old one. If you are not attracting a buyer for some reason, it is time to do a ritual for cutting the ties that bind.

 ## Ritual for selling a house

Light nine orange candles together with some incense. Nine signifies the number of Mars – precisely the energy you need to evoke to get things moving. The colour orange also signifies change and movement. Close your eyes, and ask for the custodial spirit of your home to appear in your mind's eye. See how it presents itself. Is it holding you back for some reason, or is it you who is subconsciously unwilling to leave? Perhaps you have forgotten to be grateful to the house. Receive the message in whatever way it comes. Now, write down everything that has happened (both negative and positive) to you while this has been your residence. Give thanks for what you have learnt, and the progress of personal growth you have achieved by symbolically making an offering to the house. You could do this by burning some tobacco or sage in the fire, or on a charcoal block, or burying some food underneath a tree. You also need to write down why you wish to move on. This will clarify things in your mind, and provide a strong focus. Finally, radiate out a loving welcome to the future house owners. They are out there somewhere! By doing this you have forged a link with their higher selves, and this will bring them to your door while making your house feeling warm and inviting to them.

It is also important to clear out unwanted rubbish from the cupboards, drawers, corners, attics and cellars. This automatically frees up the energy which makes room for change to take place. You can also symbolically pack a box or suitcase which you can leave by or near the front door. As a last resort, you can paint your front door orange! If none of this works, then it is obviously not the right time for you to move. So it's time to take a look at how to enhance the magic of your home to give it – and you – a new lease of life.

# WOMAN'S MAGIC AT HOME

## Making Your Home More Magical

This section comes with a health warning! Don't get too hung up on what you do or don't do to your home. Woman's magic is concerned with bringing a sense of harmony and balance into your life and home which supports who you are and what you want to create for yourself. It should not be dictated by using a specific colour, hanging a bauble in a particularly auspicious place, or finding the right numbered house to live in. Just bear in mind that woman's magic at home is about becoming consciously aware of entering into the natural flow and rhythm of your place, which automatically affects how your environment behaves just as much as how you behave within that environment. The best way to enter into this flow is by trusting your own gut instinct. This will tell you what colour to paint your ceilings, where to hang a wind chime, or when to throw out all the furniture so you can start again.

Nevertheless, in my own experience, the magical meaning of the house numbers where I lived has always been remarkably synchronistic with what I was experiencing at the time. For example, after I returned from travelling abroad, I moved into a No. 7 for two years. This enabled me time to gather myself together to write my first book, *Notions and Potions*, and to dig far deeper into who I really was than I ever had done before. At the same time I faced extreme bouts of loneliness. In fact, I don't think I'd ever felt so alone. The number 7 is not gregarious by any stretch of the imagination. Yet, looking back it provided me with the perfect time and space I needed to deepen my relationship with myself.

After the break-up of a relationship, I ended up living in a No. 20. The gentle and congenial 2 soothed my bruised spirit, while also providing me with the much needed companionship of a great friend and her daughter while I put my heart back together. The three of us lived in perfect harmony; by another quirk of fate, her daughter was called Melody! The 0 symbolises untapped potential which enabled me not only to start again, but also to make important decisions about how I wanted my life to evolve.

I now live in a home numbered 39. It provides me with the creativity of the 3 which feeds my writing and general love of life, plus the humanitarian and philanthropic qualities of the 9. I am a personal development teacher and facilitator of the Hoffman process – and known for having a love of drama in more ways than one!

Bearing all this in mind, let's now have a look at the magical significance of house numbers.

## House numbers

### NO. 1

No. 1 is governed by the life force of the sun. It stands for independence, the development of ideas and the courage to follow them through. It also represents the ego and selfishness so lessons concerning those issues will probably arise. But it's a perfect number for people who want to run their own show in some way and for those who want to get ahead.

### NO. 2

No. 2 is the number of the moon. It stands for harmony, social enjoyment, co-operation and companionship. Since it soothes the aggressive spirit, for people who want to be out there and at it, it can cause frustration. It is much more suited to people who like a gentle, congenial way of life, those who wish for nurturing, intimate partnerships, and who love to pass the time of day snoozing in hammocks.

### NO. 3

No. 3 is ruled by Jupiter. This is the number of creativity and friendship, lots of comings and goings, and extravagance. It's a perfect number for people who are writers, actors, entrepreneurs and general show-offs. It also loves romance in all sorts of shapes and sizes, so lessons of prudence, trust and loyalty may need to be learnt.

## NO. 4

No. 4 is influenced by Uranus. This is the number of discipline, will, purpose and construction – and does not like the boat being rocked. It makes an excellent number as a stable family house, and for those who enjoy a steady approach to life or who are building up a sound business. This number is not about excitement, however, so is not ideal for those who are fortune seekers, gamblers or risk-takers.

## NO. 5

No. 5 falls under the jurisdiction of Mercury. This is the number of adventure and communication which carries a banner declaring 'variety is well and truly the spice of life', therefore it is most suited to those who have loads of irons in as many different fires as possible. It also indicates travel and movement so is perfect for all who welcome the world with open arms. It can be very contrary and irresponsible, however, yet is often the number associated with fame or notoriety.

## NO. 6

No. 6 is affiliated with Venus. It is the number of the family, comfort, graciousness and beauty but also represents duty and responsibility. People who want a steady way of life, and who enjoy being of service to the community will particularly benefit. However, there could be a danger that too much is expected by kith and kin which can lead to stressful situations. Yet 6 is the number of the voice, and therefore highly beneficial for anyone interested in a singing career.

## NO. 7

No. 7 is influenced by Neptune. This is the number for spiritual purpose, contemplation and higher learning, therefore it is most appropriate for those who wish for peace and quiet, and a time for reflection. It also attracts learning and education associated with personal development of some sort. It is very nurturing for those who love their own company, are self-motivated and have their spiritual growth as a focus, but a nightmare to those who cannot live by themselves.

## NO. 8

No. 8 is governed by Saturn. This is the number of self-mastery, importance, success and abundance. It's a very powerful number for business and commerce but it does like to flaunt itself and therefore there is a tendency for these homes to be show-pieces rather than comfort zones. It is perfect for highly ambitious people who love a glamorous lifestyle, and in particular for sporting enthusiasts. It is also the number of divine law, so some sort of karmic situation may manifest which will need to be sorted out.

## NO. 9

No. 9 is influenced by Mars. This is the number of humanity, compassion and drama. Never a dull moment in fact. It loves all forms of art and entertainment as well as being drawn to a deep interest in philosophy. It's the type of home which has its door ever open, and a pot of something constantly brewing on the stove. It is perfect for those who are artistic, or possess a philanthropic approach to life, but not conducive to the more retiring types.

If your house number is a combination of numbers, look up each one for a broad picture, then add the numbers together to find the predominant influence (0 has no numerical bearing, but carries an 'all or nothing' numerological quality!). For example, no. 158 contains the determination to get ahead (1), coupled with a love of communication (5), and the power to attract abundance (8). Add together 1+5+8=14. Now add 1+4=5. 5 is the predominant influence, so the energy of this home would be led by some form of communication. My friend lived at this number while she was a television presenters' agent! She left her job as soon as she moved.

## Making a magical threshold

Your front door represents the doorway between your outer life and inner life. It is also, of course, the portal through which others enter into your inner world and therefore it is important for it to appear inviting. It is also a symbol of how you deal with issues in your life. Perhaps, for example, you struggle to open the door because the key keeps jamming in the lock. This would indicate that you tend to create unnecessary problems for yourself. Alternatively, you may have to clamber over things to get in at all, which implies that you have to fight for anything you want. It is most important to have a door which opens easily and with style. If it doesn't, it's time to fix it because when you can't gain easy access to your home, on some level you are feeling unworthy of having the peace, safety and nurturing you deserve.

It's easy to introduce a touch of magic to your front door. You just need to invest a little time, energy and love into it to bring it alive. Most front doors are still made out of wood which can be painted or left natural. However in the old days, front doors were usually made from oak. This is because, although the thickness of the wood helped to keep the warmth in and unsavoury guests out, its magical properties also provide strength, fertility and protection to the house. I have a natural pine front door. Its magical qualities are abundance, healing, fertility and protection. Perfect for any writer! I have also chosen not to paint it because, being the romantic that I am, I like the idea of passing through wood to enter my inner sanctum. It symbolically reminds me of the ancient tree groves which once played such a major part in our mystical Celtic heritage. I will be going into the magical properties of trees in greater detail in Chapter 3, so find out what kind of wood your front door is made from, and then see what magical properties it contains. Becoming aware of information like this is what sets the magic alive again.

## THRESHOLD GUARDIANS

For generations, people have been using some sort of magical protector to guard their thresholds and to ward off evil: from strings of garlic and runic symbols, to giant edifices and religious icons. I have an animal totem standing guard beside mine. It's a stone duck! Ducks happen to be my favourite birds and, to me, they represent family, stability and a lot of enjoyment, so I am very happy to have it there. There are all sorts of symbols you can put beside or over your front door to act as its guardian such as a Green Man symbol, an angel, gargoyle, a prayer or a house blessing, or stones and crystals which mean something to you. You can also find special animal door knockers, bell pulls or door handles. Dolphins are a popular choice; according to Native American Indian traditions they represent the breath of life itself. Or you could always choose your Chinese astrological sign as your guardian. But for those of us who embrace the old ways of woman's magic, animal images such as hares, cats, horses, snakes, ravens and toads are particularly relevant because of their association with the Goddess. In fact, there's not a wise woman worth her salt who doesn't live with some kind of familiar. I also plant special flower tubs beside my door because I like growing magic. I will be explaining the power of flower magic in Chapter 3.

At the end of the day, however, it's down to personal taste, so just go with what you feel makes your front door more appealing and welcoming. Changing its colour could well do the trick.

## COLOURS

Colour carries magical significance so the colour of your front door can have quite a impact on what goes on inside the home. As with anything in life, colours also contain negative and positive influences which become more pronounced the brighter the colour.

*Red* represents a passion for life and sex which is perfect for those who want lots of excitement, heated debate and a house full of people, but it can also create quarrelsome or unsettled atmospheres. *Orange* represents change and movement, so this is not a great colour if you want quiet, but it's wonderful if you want to sell your house quickly! *Yellow* represents sunshine and vitality. Perfect if you're a high energy person with a demanding lifestyle, however not advisable if you are the retiring type. *Green* represents abundance and fertility which is great for people working from home or wishing for a large family, but be cautious if you need to curb the cheque book. *Blue* is the colour of healing. It is very calming but since it also represents communication, it can indicate a house where rather a lot of gossiping takes place. *Purple* represents the more spiritual aspects of life, so is not a great colour if you want to throw endless parties. However it will certainly benefit those who want to pursue home study of some kind. *White* represents new beginnings but is also associated with nit-picking and is not a particularly inviting colour. *Black* absorbs negativity and provides protection, but it can also make your home feel invisible or nebulous in some way. *Brown* represents groundedness but it can also mean getting bogged down in the mundane side of life.

You can apply these rules to any rooms you want to paint too. Just remember that pastel shades are soothing and healing; vivid colours stimulate and activate. You can always brighten up a corner by using vivid colour in splashes with coloured candles, silk flowers or colourful china.

## Making a sacred home

Finally, any woman who loves her magical home will have a stash of incense sticks and an array of coloured candles to add ambience every moment of the day. Lighting a few candles, together with a stick of incense, instantly turns the drabbest room into a temporary temple.

I would also recommend that you create some sort of altar or sacred space and encourage your children to do the same. This is where you (and they) can spend a few moments each day just being at one with something which is special. I have a table in my sitting room on which sit spiritual icons and figurines from all kinds of different religions. I have a candle burning among them too which I light as a gesture to bring healing to the rifts which have been set up between them by the folly of human ego. I call upon these spiritual mentors to grant healing to anyone who may need it, or for my own clarity when things have gone a bit foggy inside. I also have a large stone Buddha near my fireplace. His peaceful countenance affects everyone who comes into the room. I put lighted candles in front of him when I hear about natural disasters, when a child has gone missing, there has been a dreadful massacre, or when, yet again, the planet is on the brink of war. Gestures like these are important because loving, compassionate thoughts do make a difference.

I also hang rainbow crystals to catch the sunshine so they produce a myriad of colour all over the house. People love to see them, and I often stop what I am doing just to be bathed in the rainbows. It feels healing and energising. Likewise, I hang chimes in doorways so there is always a magical tinkling going on some-where. It's simple things like this which make the house feel as if it does indeed have its own magic. And lastly I always create magic in my bathroom by bathing in candlelight and soaking in essential oils. Essential oils bring the magic of flowers and herbs into the home, and their aromas possess such powerful healing properties that they should be available on the NHS!

## Honouring your possessions

We live in a society which is driven by consumerism and the temptation to swamp ourselves with unnecessary clutter is ever present. I used be a terrible hoarder – in fact I would spend entire weekends ferreting around in car boots and jumble sales. But as I became more in tune with my real needs, I began to realise that the adage 'less is more' certainly rings true. As soon as I began to free myself of those unnecessary trappings and only kept items which supported the type of spiritual life I wanted to manifest, it felt as if a ton of weight lifted from my shoulders.

I still love going to car boots and auction rooms because I would rather go on the romance of a treasure hunt than buy new, but this now only occurs when I need something special. In which case I enlist the help of my 'shopping guide'; my shopping guide and I have developed a very successful and fun relationship over the years! I just focus on the item I want, then ask my shopping guide to help me locate it. This is a typical story:

I wanted an old stone bird bath to put outside my study win-dow because I couldn't imagine a more delightful distraction than watching birds enjoy a good splash. I put the intent to my guide, and then left it with him. A couple of weeks later, I had an over-whelming compulsion to go to a local auction which I had only been to once before. There, hidden among all sorts of bits and bobs, was my bird bath, the style and age of which fulfilled every expectation! It was as if my guide had done the footwork, and then given me the nudge and wink. Consequently, every time I look at it, it fills me with a sense of magic and wonderment – and naturally there is a large label of thanks hanging on my tree of gratitude.

Everything in my home means something special to me and I have chosen not to be bogged down by family heirlooms unless they truly enhance my spiritual path. I also get rid anything I don't use, and that includes unwanted gifts. I give thanks to the spirit of the gift, and then it goes straight down to a local charity shop for the benefit of someone else. I don't have a big wardrobe either because how many clothes do you really need? Anything which hasn't been worn for a while also gets hauled off to the charity shop.

I regard my plants as house companions, and always wish them good morning and thank them for bringing life into the house. I also give grateful thanks to my car every time it starts so effortlessly, as well as my dear old washing machine and, of course, my computer. Without these treasures, my life would not be able to flow with such ease. Thus my home is full of things which feel like friends, and which act as a reminder of how incredibly fortunate I am. It is a great pleasure to wake up among them each morning, and feel so completely loved and supported.

I will finish this section by saying *when you begin to consciously breathe magic into your home, it will automatically breathe the magic right back into you!*

# Chapter 3
# Woman's Magic
# in the Garden

Let food be your medicine
Let medicine be your food

*Hippocrates (5th century BC)*

**THERE IS NO GREATER JOY** for me than lying down on the grass, arms outstretched on a summer's day, eyes closed, listening to the birds singing from the depths of their souls, and feeling the tickle of a beetle scurrying by. Sometimes I do this just to feel the sheer pleasure of the earth underneath me and, at other times, when I feel I have lost my way a little and need to rejuvenate my spirits. The physical feeling of being so totally connected with this great planet and all that is in it always makes me feel better. I also sense an extraordinary power surging through me as I attune to the Earth Goddess to ask for her blessing, and for help and guidance too when necessary. Surrendering to the earth frees me from stress, and all manner of aches and pains. It is as if the earth is washing my psyche clean, transmuting any negativity into something which supports and nourishes me.

Nature is one enormous natural healing remedy. It is no accident that the sky is blue and nature is predominantly green. Blue is the colour of healing and communication while green opens and soothes the heart. It offers no practical solutions to any of our problems, yet its passive state provides us with the ultimate gift of being completely receptive to any mood we may be in. I can remember once being very low – nothing was going right,

49

and I felt unsupported and lonely. I went for a long walk which led to a large, beautiful, tranquil pond. I sat down on a stone, put my feet into the water and then poured out my heart and tears to it. Although the pond just carried on being a pond, I felt that not only was I was being received and held in some way, but that I had also been truly heard with unconditional acceptance. The inner healing and peace I found from this encounter was incredible. I also learnt a profound lesson on how to listen. Become a pond.

My pond experience took place a day before a massive life-changing crisis which catapulted me on to my healing path. As I began to unravel the layers of non-me in which I had been enveloped, I began to look more and more towards nature to help me answer the question of who I really was. This is turn led me to study Native American Indian practices and suddenly I understood that without becoming one with the natural world, we are lost souls. Within a very short space of time I realised living in a city environment was slowly killing my spirit, so after twenty years I moved out to the country. From then on, I began to feel as if I belonged to the earth, as much as the earth belonged in me. I also began to discover the existence of the devic realms, and that's when life became truly magical.

## The Devic Realms

There are four devic realms – earth, air, fire and water – which contain etheric elemental spirits or sprites. There is nothing new or weird about this. People have been painting pictures and writing about these devic realms for hundreds of years, albeit sometimes thinly disguised through children's fantasy stories, including Tolkein's *Lord of the Rings*. Members of the famous spiritual centre of Findhorn in Scotland wrote a book about how they worked with the devic realms to create a magnificent garden on virtually barren land. The devas taught them where to plant specific vegetables, herbs and flowers, and what each required for it to thrive and produce the most succulent of foods. Indigenous cultures also work with the devic realms and create great ceremonies to celebrate the importance of their existence, and to give thanks to them for helping maintain the health and spiritual welfare of the people. We in the Western world are forgetting this magic. The consequence of this is an awful disrespect for the land, and the destruction of virtually all our sacred and hallow ground. The essence of the world will never be destroyed, no matter what humans do to it, but we will destroy ourselves unless we learn to live in harmony with nature again. As part of all our healing processes it is important to look at the beauty which surrounds us with true appreciation, and to open ourselves up to the magic which resides within it.

The four devic realms act as custodians for the elements of earth, air, fire and water. Each of these elements is affiliated with one of the four directions:

Earth: **north** the realm of the gnomes
Air: **east** the realm of the sylphs
Fire: **south** the realm of the salamanders
Water: **west** the realm of the undines

In native customs, as well as in the practice of the old ways, the four directions and their elemental realms are laid out in a circle which symbolises the eternal passage of existence: what we put out comes back to us at some point along our earthly cycles because there is no beginning and no end to life as such. In the old ceremonies and traditions, each realm is represented symbolically. This is also illustrated by the four minor arcana suits of the tarot.

# The Gnomes of Earth and the North: the Suit of Pentacles

The gnomes are guardians of winter, the direction of the north, the physical world and of fertility and abundance. The north is traditionally known as the gateway to inner wisdom. The earth provides us with food – and an abundance of beauty without which our souls would simply curl up and die. The gnomes are also custodians of everything that grows, from tiny flowers to giant trees. I had a wonderful experience with a gnome when I began to work with the earth's elemental realms. Together with a friend, I conducted a thank-you ritual for the gnomes in my garden because it was such a beautiful place to be. I wanted to make sure that the gnomes were also welcome in the house so I lit a candle for them, sent a prayer of thanks, and left an offering of food overnight by the fireplace. The next day several friends came to lunch. Before lunch we gathered in the sitting room to have a few drinks and then moved *en masse* into the kitchen, leaving the sitting room door ajar. During lunch my friend and I told our guests about the gnome ritual and a good laugh was had by all. However, after we had finished lunch we found that the sitting room door had magically locked itself from the inside! One of my guests had to break the lock on the door to get in and all of us knew instantly that this trick had been played on us by my gnomes! My garden went on to produce the most wonderful vegetables and flowers I have ever had, and I always felt as if some sort of presence was accompanying me whenever I went outside.

## Giving thanks to the gnome elementals

It's best to do this outside, either in the garden or a quiet place in the countryside. If neither are possible, then you can work with pot plants, a bowl of fruit or a wonderful bunch of flowers. You could also use the Ace of Pentacles from the tarot pack as a symbol to meditate on.

Sit comfortably – I enjoy nestling into the trunk of a tree. Close your eyes, and relax. Allow all your tension to drain into the earth beneath you, or into the strength of the tree behind you. Open your heart to the sounds of nature, and surrender to its magnificence. In your mind's eye call your inner wise woman to manifest before you. She is your ancient teacher of the healing powers of the old ways. When you are ready, allow her to take you by the hand as she guides you into the depths of the earth. She takes you towards an ancient wooden door which magically opens. Through this door is the realm of the gnomes who come to greet you with great excitement and joy. They want to tell you about themselves, and the role they play in creating abundance through the earth. Allow them to take you on an adventure of discovery. Suddenly you feel as if you have become the soil itself, providing nourishment for plants and animals alike. And now you are a field of corn ripening in the sun; the branches of an ancient oak tree; a tiny seed germinating; and a dense forest. Feel what it is like to grow roots deep into the soil, and to experience the changing seasons. At the end of this journey, the gnomes give you a profound teaching message which you can make use of in your daily life. Pay homage and give thanks to these elemental gnomes, and make a vow that you will continue to cherish all living things. Allow your inner wise woman to escort you back to the surface of the earth, and after you have given thanks, open your eyes. See if the world feels different, or if you notice something different about the nature which surrounds you. Leave a small token of appreciation for them.

Get into the habit of giving thanks to the countryside as you walk through it, of picking up litter, and of blessing the spirits of hedges and trees which are being hacked down by hedge-cutters or chainsaws. I also bless the spirit of any dead animal I see which may have been killed by a passing car. By this act alone, you will feel a sense of belonging to this wonderful realm and that you are giving something positive back to it.

# The Sylphs of Air and the East: the Suit of Swords

The sylphs are guardians of spring, the direction of the east and the wind. Therefore they are expressly concerned with communication, the mind, the intellect and the kingdom of the feathered creatures. The east is the doorway to new beginnings, and the direction through which the sacred circle is always entered. Air, and its various components, is our vital life force – it enables us to exist within the atmosphere of this particular planet. It makes its presence felt through its four winds: the north brings cold and 'death'; the east brings freshness and new life; the south brings warmth and vitality; and the west brings fertility and gentle persuasion. It also supports that which flies – including human-made technology as well as the bird fraternity. Its clouds give us rain for our crops to grow and thrive, and for our rivers and oceans to be replenished, while its clear skies provide sunshine for nature to ripen, and for humans to bask in. It allows candles to burn and for communication to flow with ease. It also stimulates our intellect so we know how to be granted good reason and acts of justice.

## Giving thanks to the sylphs

Find a tall tree to sit beneath so you can hear the wind rustling through its leaves. If this is not convenient, light an incense stick and meditate on its smoke rising to the ceiling. Smoke is also a symbol of air. You can concentrate on the Ace of Swords from the tarot pack.

Let your eyes gently close and enjoy entering into the centre of the wind which is caressing the branches of your tree. In your mind's eye, allow yourself to become the wind, and feel what it is like to mingle and toy with the leaves, and to make the trunk sway at your whim. Now ask for your wise woman to appear, and allow her to lead you into the very heart of the wind (or smoke). In the midst of it, a great cloud appears which opens effortlessly to reveal the innermost world of the sylphs. They welcome you into their domain and whip you off into an incredible adventure. you see the world through their eyes; how storms and clouds are formed, how clarity comes by the wind suddenly changing direction, and how messages are conveyed to distant places by it. See how this affects your intellectual thinking. You can also explore how a bird soars through the air or uses thermals to raise itself higher. See the importance of clean air, and of the effect that pollution is having on the earth. Become aware of the battle that the sylphs are having through the ignorance of humankind.

At the end of this journey, the sylphs give you a profound teaching message which you can make use of in your daily life. Pay homage and give thanks to these airy creatures, and make a vow that you will respect and revere the environment in which you live. Allow your inner wise woman to escort you back to your tree and, after you have given thanks for your vision, open your eyes. Notice anything which may appear different and leave a small token of your appreciation for them.

Get into the habit of being aware of the wind bringing messages to you, that birds are the embodiment of sylphs, and of blessing aeroplanes as they pass overhead. I have never enjoyed travelling in planes, so whenever I see an aeroplane overhead, I always send the passengers and crew thoughts for a good flight and joy for their journeys. It doesn't matter that they are oblivious of this, what matters is that you are doing it. Everyone on those planes will be affected in some way for their highest good.

# The Salamander of Fire and the South: the Suit of Wands

The salamanders are the guardians of summer and fire; this is the realm of inspiration, sexual passion, change and the inner child. Fire provides us with warmth on cold winter nights, fuel for cooking and heating water, and also voraciously destroys the old so new life can spring forth out of the ashes. It is the essence from which the phoenix arises. Fire is also the representation of the inner child – the place of innocence where we have all come from. As it gives rise to sexual fervour it is also the root of our creative spirit and it is from here that those *euikas* come, and where important signs manifest. These have, on occasions, literally changed the course of humankind – think about Moses and the burning bush. The salamanders can be seen in the heart of fires, dancing like dragons. This dragon symbology is used in many Eastern religions to pay homage to them.

## Giving thanks to the salamanders

I love this realm because it means giving myself time to enjoy the luxury of being mesmerised by those flickering flames, often for hours. Many strange things can appear in the heart of a fire – visions which are prophetic, inspiring or which carry powerful messages. Fire magic is extremely potent too since you can use it to burn away the old, or draw in the new. You can also use the Ace of Wands as its symbology.

This gratitude ritual can either be done outside by building a bonfire, inside with a hearth fire or by using the flame of a candle. If you are in a room, turn off all the lights so the room is just lit by the fire. The effect is quite magical.

Look into the flames, and allow yourself to relax completely. Let the flames take over your mind until it feels as if you have stepped into the heart of the fire. Feel yourself dancing and flickering with them, becoming one with the dragon energy. Now see your wise woman appear beside you and allow her to escort you through a great flaming door into the world of the salamanders, the ancient fiery ones. Allow them to gather you up into their flaming folds and take you on a great journey of discovery. Feel the intense heat of a house ablaze, the crack of a thunderbolt as it sets a tree alight, or a forest suddenly catching alight. Now feel the warmth of a gentle hearth and of something delicious cooking over an open fire. See how the salamanders create inspiration in our minds and how our creative instincts are borne by them. You can also climb on their great fire dragon backs and allow yourself to be taken on a ride of a lifetime.

At the end of this journey, the salamanders give you a profound teaching message which you can make use of in your daily life. Pay homage and give thanks to these fiery creatures, and make a vow that you will now pay homage to the salamanders whenever you receive a inspirational thought. Allow your inner wise woman to escort you back to your own fire and, after you have given thanks for your vision, open your eyes. Notice anything which may appear different and leave a small token of your appreciation for your salamanders.

The flame is the universal symbol of light, so light candles on a daily basis to send thoughts to someone or somewhere in the world which needs healing or help. We need to spread as much of this light as we possibly can.

# The Undines of Water and the West: the Suit of Cups

The undines govern the realm of autumn and water; secrets of the dream time, of inner visions, emotions and journeys. In many religions, water symbolises initiation through baptism in the waters of life, as well as representing 'the great river of life'. The ferryman comes to carry us across to the afterlife when our time is done. In old times all the great rivers were considered sacred and holy, for without water nothing can prosper. The Ganges plays a central role in Hindu worship for this very reason. Springs, wells, pools and fountains were also considered to be holy places where great healing properties could be found and prophecies foretold. Water cults still exist today such as at Lourdes which has six million visitors a year, and Zamzam, the spring in the centre of Mecca which is worshipped by millions of Muslims as part of their Haj pilgrimage. We are made from 75 per cent water which acts as a channel or 'stream' for all physical and chemical changes to take place. As we age, we naturally dehydrate, losing approximately 10 per cent of our body fluid – causing us to appear as if we are shrinking. Three-quarters of the world's surface is covered by seas and oceans. These are governed by the pull of the moon which produces a natural rhythmical heartbeat for the entire world.

Water is the most precious commodity which the earth has, and it has been suggested that as the world progresses it will become more valuable than oil. Folklore says that water gives to us what we give to it. The pollution which we pour into our rivers and oceans is insidiously destroying the animal life it sustains, as well as our own. We have to take more responsibility for it if our world is to prosper in future generations. The undines need our help.

## Giving thanks to the undines

We all love to sit by a gentle waterfall, or listen to the babbling of a stream or brook. So if it's possible, find a safe place out in nature beside a river, or in your garden by a fountain. Alternatively at home, you could fill a bowl with water and place a flower or floating candle in it. Water is represented by the Ace of Cups in the tarot.

Close your eyes, or allow yourself to become mesmerised by the flowing movement of the water. Feel it washing over you, cleansing your mind and spirit of any negative thoughts or emotions. Let yourself enter into its rhythm and flow and feel as if you have become part of the water itself. See what it feels like to wash over pebbles and rocks, for fish to swim within you and for plants to grow. Now see your wise woman appear, and allow her to escort you to a magnificent waterfall through which you pass into the realm of the undines. The undines welcome you with glee and suddenly you are darting with them in the great waters of life. Allow yourself to become the ocean, full of schools of whales and dolphins, and shoals of tiny fish. You feel the muffled noise of a tanker passing through your waters, and of a yacht sailing by. Now you are a mighty river in full flood, destroying everything in your path, and now a small river teaming with life. You are also a puddle

on the ground and the drip from a tap, a drop of rain
falling on to a flower and a menacing thunderstorm. And
now you are the gentle lapping of the sea on the shore, a
long drink of water to quench a thirst and a sacred holy
place which is full of healing properties. The undines show
you how your own body is made up predominantly of
water and what your body needs to sustain itself. You are
shown your emotional realm and how you inherently
respond to things which happen around you. Finally the
undines take you into the realms of your inner vision and
dreams.

At the end of your journey, the undines give you a
profound teaching message which you can make use of in
your daily life. Pay homage and give thanks to these watery
creatures, and make a vow that you will now pay homage
to the undines whenever you receive an inner vision or
prophetic dream. Allow your inner wise woman to escort
you back to your own stream and, after you have given
thanks for your vision, open your eyes. Notice anything
which may appear different and leave a small token of your
appreciation for your undines.

Becoming consciously aware of the element of water and its extraordinary healing properties means that we begin to pay attention
to our own water intake. You should try to drink at least 1 to 2
litres of fresh water a day. You can also bless tap water as you drink
it to raise its vibrations, and place essential oils into your bath to
invigorate or relax yourself. But, above all, encourage everyone
you know to take care of this precious element. Without water we
have nothing.

# WOMAN'S MAGIC IN THE GARDEN
## Herbalism

Now we have explored the magical devic realms let's have a look at what they produce for us to enjoy.

Herbs, plants and trees have always been used as potent cure-alls as well as providing us with food, but they also have magical properties. Herbs and plants have been used in all sorts of ways to draw in love, provide protection, create abundance, keep a lover faithful, send messages of healing out into the world and so on. In the old traditions of the wise crafts, the use of these wonderful plants is traditionally known as 'wort cunning'. *Wort* comes from the Old English *wyrt* meaning plant or herb. The word *cunning* refers to employing a skill in a shrewd or wise way. Therefore wort cunning literally means herbal knowledge. A vestige of this old practice has been preserved in such wonderful plant names as figwort, mugwort and St John's wort.

### Herbalism through history

The earliest written record of the practice of herbalism was by the Chinese emperor Shen Nung, called *The Great Herbal*. This contained details of at least 365 plants and herbs and dates back around 3,000 years. Another source was found in Egypt, dated c.2,500 BC and this provides hieroglyphic evidence of the important part herbs and plants played in the health and spiritual welfare of the people and their religion. The Bible is also peppered with references to all manner of herbs, plants and fruits. Such was their importance that many were used as powerful religious symbols. Examples are: 'I am the vine' as in John's gospel, and in Exodus it clearly describes the hems of priests' robes being embroidered with pomegranates, the sacred fruits of Persephone, Queen of the Underworld, which symbolised the subconscious mind and life beyond the great divide. The magical significance of these delicious and exotic fruits was also associated with fertility and good luck and therefore many households hung them over their doorways to guard against evil. Honeysuckle was grown around the front porch to ward off fevers. Rue was used as a protection against the evil eye, and many old wives' tales speak of the benefits of placing rue in the home as a protection against psychic attack, as well as for healing a broken heart. Herbal magic played a central role in mythological legends too. Medea, for example, the daughter of the Greek king Colchis, was renowned for her skills in magic which helped Jason to win the golden fleece.

During their occupation, the Romans did much to spread the word about the medicinal, magical and culinary uses of herbs and plants throughout Europe by creating massive herb gardens which they needed to treat their troops and to appease their gods. Among other plants, they introduced rosemary, thyme, basil, sage and garlic to Europe. However, with the decline of the Roman Empire and the subsequent rise of Christianity, the church, in an effort to gain control of its people, hindered and often forbade the study of science, which included research into herbal medicine. Invaluable sources of medicinal research were destroyed, and the great medical school of Alexander was razed to the ground. With it, over 7,000 books were destroyed.

Yet it was through the extensive gardens created by various monastic orders which came into being during this time that the wisdom of herbalism continued to thrive all over Europe. However, this was at great cost to the old Druid order since monasteries and churches were usually established on sacred Druid sites specifically to destroy the old ways of the ancient religions. Up until then the Druids were reverently acclaimed as the keepers of the sacred lores of earth magic whose practices celebrated the mysteries of life. Indeed, the word *druid* means *knowledge of the oak* – a tree of great strength, hardiness, durability and longevity. The task of the Druids was to maintain the delicate balance between the seen and unseen worlds, with precious and sacred oak groves being the focal point of their ceremonies.

At the same time as the monks were establishing their stronghold throughout Europe, the witch hunts came into full swing. Many innocent women were subject to appalling persecution. Most were simply local wise women whose knowledge of herbal lore and healing undermined the professional healers of the times – namely male doctors and clergymen who had set themselves up as exclusive authorities on medicine even though they had little training or understanding of the subtle and mystical energies of plants and herbs. This persecution broke the lineage of female healers, yet the knowledge was kept alive by passing it down in secret from mother to daughter. Herbs and plants continued to thrive because they were also used as ingredients in perfumes and cosmetics, insect repellent and much-needed aromatic scents in the house. In addition, herbs such as bergamot, balm, hyssop, lavender, thyme and savory were cultivated especially to attract bees since honey was the only source of sweetener in those days. Thyme was also used as an astringent to kill bugs in meat.

Over the ensuing years, apothecaries and pharmacies sprang up in abundance to cater for the common people. The word *pharmacy* comes from the Greek *pharmakeia* which means the making of magical potions and philters (charms or drugs), as well as compounding medical drugs. However their existence incited great jealousy among the many surgeons and doctors who vied with each other for the custom of the ailing. In England pressure was put to bear for their closure until King Henry VIII stepped in. He was a keen herbalist himself and quickly realised that if herbal medicine was to be monopolised by the medical fraternity, it would prevent him from using it as he pleased. He therefore passed an Act of Parliament decreeing that it was lawful for anyone in his kingdom to practise the craft of herbalism – a law which is still upheld in the British Isles today.

During the Second World War, herbal medicine went into serious decline due to the growth of the pharmaceutical industry which began to influence all areas of health and healing. Medicines were needed in huge amounts and because it was difficult to meet the demand via traditional herbal remedies, great in-roads were made into pharmaceutical exploration. New wonder drugs (the word *drug* originates from an old English word *drogges*, literally meaning dried roots) such as penicillin swamped the market as a more immediately effective method for treating infections. And so began the great divide between traditional herbal healing and modern medicine.

Pharmaceutical companies now well and truly have the power with regard to our health and welfare. As they research the healing components of plants and herbs, they patent what they discover so no one else is allowed to use it. This means that there is a real danger of herbalism being pushed underground again. However, for those of us who love plants, our gardens will always continue to be a source of wonderment, healing and magic. Home herbalism costs virtually nothing and is safe and easy to practise providing you follow simple guidelines. As with any treatment, if you are pregnant or taking regular medication always consult your doctor before use.

## Wort cunning and the doctrine of signatures

Herbalism uses the whole plant for healing which is much safer because there are fewer side effects. Plant properties act completely differently when chemicals are isolated, or components or compounds separated or purified as in modern medicines. For example, the pharmaceutically produced aspirin which comes mainly from meadowsweet can have the side effect of causing stomach ulcers.

The whole plant, however, is used in herbalism to cure stomach ulcers. Herbalism works on the subtle etheric bodies which include physical, emotional, mental and spiritual aspects. The remedies gently activate and, although slower to take effect, they are much more effective in the long run than pharmaceutical drugs which usually suppress symptoms rather than curing the cause. Herbal medicine allows the root cause of the disease to surface, so symptoms can appear to worsen before they get better. It usually takes up to six weeks for the medicinal effect of a herb to kick in, so stay with it.

The magical and medicinal properties of plants and trees were discovered through observing their shape, texture and perfume. This became known as the doctrine of signatures. For example, the willow bends in the wind. Its bark was discovered to contain certain healing properties which are used to aid suppleness in joints. The tiny heart-shaped leaves of the plant heartsease are used in magic to heal a wounded heart. The brain-shaped leaves of the ginko tree are used to restore memory and the circulation of the brain. Perhaps the most occult doctrine of signatures belongs to spindle or wahoo which grows naturally in hedgerows and was considered to be one of the sacred herbs of the Druids. In the old days, woodcutters never cut spindle since they believed it would bring bad luck. This is because it was used to make spindles for weaving and was therefore affiliated with woman's magic and the magic of the Goddess herself who weaves the web of the universe.

You can also make up your own magical doctrine of signatures by meditating with a plant, and asking for its spirit to give you its secrets. Many herbalists affiliate their plants with astrological influence as well as the four elemental powers. Remember that this includes what we call weeds. Many of our weeds provide us with incredibly powerful healing remedies such as cleavers which are used to aid the digestive system, and common ground ivy which is used to treat catarrhal conditions while also possessing the magical properties of drawing in good luck, fidelity and love.

The practice of wort cunning comes, however, with a serious warning. **Do not eat or drink any part of any plant** unless you know what you are dealing with. Some plants are highly toxic and can cause death. The rules of herbalism are:

**1** Look at and smell a plant first. Reject it if it has a repellent odour, or if you instinctively feel that it is poisonous.

**2** Rub a small piece of the plant on to your inner arm. If there is a reaction, it could well be poisonous.

**3** If there is no reaction, rub a small piece of the plant on to your outer lip. If it starts to burn, wash it off immediately because it is probably poisonous.

**4** If, after twenty-four hours, there is no reaction, rub a small bit on your inner lip. Leave for twenty-four hours.

**5** If no reaction, chew a small bit and then spit it out. Leave for forty-eight hours.

**6** If no reaction, swallow a tiny piece and leave for a week. Gradually increase the intake of the plant until you are sure you are not suffering any adverse reactions.

## Women's 'still rooms'

Herbal magic has always been associated with women's mysteries because in bygone times she was the mistress of the household, as well as being the nurse, doctor, midwife, cook and, of course, mother. It was also she who would make the necessary perfumes and concoctions to protect the household and linens from bugs, to battle with unpleasant smells, and to make sure the health of her family was maintained as far as possible. Elizabethan women created special 'still rooms' or small distilleries to make oils and perfumes, where bunches of flowers would be hung to dry for medicines as well as for making magic in secret, and where a number of spices and fixatives would be kept to make pot pourris to sweeten rooms, together with perfumed vinegars which were sprinkled on rush flooring. Exotic spices came to Britain through the silk routes, and would include such delicacies as myrrh, frankincense and sandalwood. These oils were used to fumigate the house or to keep sickness from spreading.

The word *perfume* comes from the Latin *through smoke*, because originally perfumed oil was burnt as an offering of appeasement to the gods. The perfumed smoke acted as a messenger to the gods as it rose to the heavens. Magic was also interwoven into the use of oils, and it is said that Helen of Troy was granted her beauty through a perfume mixture given to her by Venus, the Goddess of Love. Women used oils particularly as aphrodisiacs, to weave spells over their men to keep them faithful, or to help seduce their prey! It was said that Cleopatra had the floors of her palace strewn knee-deep with rose petals as an incitement for both Caesar and Mark Anthony; and apparently she had her sail washed in perfumed water on state occasions as she sailed down the Nile.

## Harvesting to the rhythm of the moon

Traditionally, herbs which are used for both medicinal and magical purposes are best when gathered before midday in dry weather, during the waxing or full moon and cut with a knife made from a silver blade with a black handle. (Silver is the moon's own metal, and the black handle represents dark mystery.) This is because the water content of the plant is at its height and in harmony with the high tides of the oceans. Therefore, they are more succulent, energised and, of course, potent. Since the human body contains over 70 per cent water, our emotions and psychic abilities also become more acute and more receptive to the qualities and properties of the plants.

Leaves need to be gathered just before the flowers come. Pick flowers before they open, and seeds and fruits as they ripen, or when they come easily into your hand. Roots need to be gathered when everything above the ground is 'dead'. This is either in autumn when the juices return to the root or early spring as the root begins to energise with life again.

## Planting to the rhythm of the moon

Planting also needs to be done during the waxing phase of the moon. This ensures that the ground is at its most potent to receive and support new life. Make sure you bless your seeds as you plant them, and consciously place them in the protection of the gnomes as well as the loving embrace of the Goddess. This automatically raises their potency while also making them even more magical. It is especially important when planting vegetable seeds. The blessings you sow, you will also reap in more ways than you can imagine, and your vegetables will taste truly divine.

## Making your own magical herbal oils

This is very easy to do. You just need a window shelf which catches the sun, a clean brown bottle in which is placed a carrier oil such as almond or grape oil and a handful of flowers or herbs which vibrate to the magical qualities you want to draw into your life.

Put the flower heads or herbs into the bottle of oil and seal tightly. Leave in the sunlight for thirty days, or a whole cycle of the moon. I prefer to work with the moon's cycle. You can then either distil the oil by taking out the flower heads or herbs, or leave them in the oil, depending on what you want to use it for. I would recommend that you distil the oil when making massage oils.

You can also make exotic oil mixtures by adding a few drops of essential oils to a carrier oil. Store these in a dark place. Sprinkle a few drops of your oils on your bed linen, in your underwear drawer, or even on your carpets to give your home an evocative and sensuous aroma.

## Women's herbs

Women's herbs are used to help in pregnancy, to ease child-birth, to treat irregular periods and to help with menopausal changes. Here are some plants which you can grow in your garden to make your own teas and tinctures, or buy from a specialist herb shop.

> **Agnus castus:** For irregular periods.
> **Calendula:** Very effective for any type of fungal or bacterial infection.
> **Corn silk:** A diuretic which soothes cystitis.
> **Cramp bark:** To relieve heavy periods and to soothe headaches.
> **Echinacea:** To boost the immune system and combat thrush.
> **Herb Robert:** To stop internal bleeding and for any gynaecological disorder.
> **Lady's mantle:** Improves muscle tone to the uterus and therefore cuts down the likelihood of hysterectomy when taken on a regular basis. Research shows that hysterectomies are reduced by one-third in those taking lady's mantle.
> **Lavender:** To make into a pillow to induce relaxation and sleep.
> **Milkthistle:** Affiliated to the virgin Mary and the best cure for a hangover, provided it is taken before you start drinking!

**Penny royal:** Strengthens uterine contractions and stimulates the menstruation process.

**Raspberry leaf tea** (raspberries resemble the shape of the inside of the uterus): Given by professional herbalists during last days of pregnancy to ease childbirth.

**Shepherd's purse:** To help prevent bleeding from the womb.

**Skull cap:** For soothing nervous disorders.

**Squaw vine** (Native American Indian plant): Used for preparing the uterus for childbirth.

**St John's wort:** A very successful natural replacement for Prozac.

**Yarrow:** For painful periods and to regulate menstrual cycle (to be taken as tea twice daily).

Teas are made from a handful of dried leaves, flowers and small seeds which have been finely chopped or ground by pestle and mortar. Place into boiling water and allow to steep for ten minutes. *Dose*: one cup of the warm liquid three times a day.

Tinctures are made by distilling the herbs into alcohol, such as brandy or vodka. *Dose*: drink a capful in warm water three times a day.

Decoctions are made from simmering roots, or seeds and fruits in water for at least twenty minutes. Drain, and drink one cup three times a day.

**When in doubt about any ailment, or when an ailment persists, you need to consult a qualified herbalist.**

# The Magical Qualities of Flowers

The subtle aromas of flowers act on our olfactory organs, which open up our higher centres of consciousness, providing us with waves of bliss. There are literally thousands of flowers to make magic with, and here are some of my own personal favourites, together with a little folklore.

**Cornflowers:** The Latin name, *centaurea*, comes from the mythic Centaur, the teacher of Achilles who, having hurt his foot, cured it with the juices of this flower. Cornflowers are also known as 'love in abundance' and are used in fertility rituals as well as abundance spells.

**Daisies:** Known as 'the tears of Mary' because they appear at Easter. They stand for innocence and are used to soothe away the rigours of the day, as well as to quell quarrels. They are highly recommended for use in offices to reduce stress.

**Jasmine:** Known as 'womanly sweetness' and wonderful for helping you to open up to the sensuousness of love because it puts you in touch with your sexual instincts. You can also burn jasmine oil and anoint yourself with the oil to enhance love-making. Present a jasmine plant to a man if you want to open his heart.

**Lavender:** Dedicated to Vesta and her vestal virgins, lavender comes from the Latin *to wash*. It brings honesty and directness to relationships and is used extensively in love potions. Cut the flowers during a full moon, place in olive oil and then leave in sunlight for three days. Rub yourself with the oil for purification and to rid yourself of the past.

**Lilies:** The Hebrew name Susan means 'as pure as a lily'. Lilies are dedicated to Hera, Goddess of the Sky, because, according to legend, Hercules sucked so ferociously from Hera's breasts that milk spilt from them on to the earth, from which sprung white lilies. So when a man gives a woman white lilies it means he respects her purity. The white lily also represents the souls of unborn children, and are planted as a way of making contact with them. Lilies are also used to symbolise the return to innocence of those who have died, which is why they are traditionally used for funerals.

**Roses:** Roses were made for love. Their delicate perfumes and colours open the heart to the height of romantic love and virtue. Red roses symbolise passion; pink roses represent tenderness and white are for purity. Bathe in the petals and scatter them between your sheets to bring love into your life and to enhance your love-making. You can also plant a rose bush as a symbol of your marriage vow to love. As it grows strong, so will your love. However, if it should wilt, so will your union.

**Sunflowers:** Atahualpa, God King of the Incas, had as his symbol a solid gold sunflower. The Incas believed that the sunflower possessed potent magical properties because of the intricate geometrical patterns of its flower head. The sunflower is naturally affiliated with the power of the sun and therefore masculinity. Consequently, it is used in many love spells to attract a man. It can also be used in a fire ritual to cleanse yourself of woes and worries by throwing some petals into the flames. Eating sunflower seeds can help you to gain inner power and strength.

**Tulips:** These are used to heal the heart and give to someone you have argued with because they will heal a rift. Yellow means helpless love, red are a declaration of love, and white means 'forget me not'.

**Violets:** The Romans used violets to adorn their banqueting halls because they were thought to protect against drunkenness. The dead were covered with violets as a symbol of the beauty and fragility of life. Since violets are traditionally associated with the feminine element, when you feel sad or vulnerable, buy or pick a small bunch, and allow them to share your sorrows. You can also float them in your bath to comfort you, or drink an infusion made from the leaves to soothe and calm feelings of hysteria or nervous problems.

## The traditional meanings of cottage garden flowers

Here is a list of some of the most common flowers and shrubs which grow in our gardens together with their traditional symbolism.

**Aconite** to overcome hatred
**Anemones** for expectation
**Azaleas** to find temperance
**Begonias** to chase away dark thoughts
**Belladonna** for silence
**Bleeding heart** shows a willingness to love
**Bluebells** bring constancy
**Bullrushes** for quietness and reflection
**Camomile** brings peace and harmony
**Carnation** for pure love
**Christmas rose** to relieve anxiety
**Chrysanthemums** to heal slighted love
**Clematis** to honour mental beauty
**Clover** to draw in happiness
**Crocus** for gladness
**Cyclamen** to find confidence and inner strength
**Daffodil** for regard and chivalry, and to overcome regret
**Dahlias** to overcome instability
**Ferns** for fascination
**Fleabane** to bring higher blessings
**Forget-me-not** for true love
**Foxgloves** stimulate sexual love and protect against insincerity

# WOMAN'S MAGIC

**Gardinias** to soothe anxiety

**Gloxinia** to represent a proud spirit

**Honeysuckle** for devoted affection

**Hydrangea** to protect against psychic attack

**Hyssop** for cleanliness of the body and spirit

**Iris** a message of faith, wisdom and valour

**Lilac** for the first throes of falling in love

**Lily of the valley** shows a return to happiness

**Lupins** a friend to all, veraciousnen

**Marigold** for a sunny soul

**Mugwort** to bring happiness

**Musk** for unconscious sweetness

**Narcissus** to overcome egotism

**Nasturtiums** to promote patriotism

**Orchids** a beauty to behold

**Pansies** for drawing in thoughts of love

**Passion flower** to bring calm and peace

**Peony** to overcome bashfulness

**Phlox** for unanimous union

**Poppy** to induce dreams

**Primrose** to find youthfulness

**Pyrethrums** to find forgiveness for those who have inflicted pain

**Red hot pokers** to pierce open a cold heart

**Rosebay** a warning of danger

**Saxifrage** to show affection

**Scillas** to learn forgiveness

**Snowdrops** bring hope

**Speedwell** to bring fidelity

**Star of Bethlehem** to call a reconciliation

**Sweet briar** to heal a wound

**Sweet pea** delicate pleasure

**Vervain** for enchantment

# Woman's Magic in the Garden

You can work with all the flowers in your garden to find out the special meaning they have for you. Flowers can also be made into special pot pourris which you can use to freshen up drawers and cupboards, or to put a special zing into a room where you want to draw a little magic.

## How to make magical pot pourri

Pot pourri is made from dried flower petals. (The term *pot pourri* comes from the French *rotted pot*.) If you are drying flowers from your own garden, hang them up in bunches, with flower heads downwards in a brown paper bag, in a warm, dry environment. It will take about ten days for them to dry to a crackly crispness. Combine the petals with spices and herbs of your choice and then add a few drops of essential oil to enhance the perfume. You will now need to add a fixative such as orris root (one teaspoon to every five handfuls of flowers). This absorbs the oils and keeps the petals looking fresh. Benzoin and storax are also potent fixers which you can use either individually or in combination with orris.

Put the mixture into an airtight jar for six weeks, giving it a good shake every day, while also empowering it with blessings and the type of magic you want to draw into your life. Once the six weeks are up, it is ready to be put into a bowl and placed in your home where you want the magic to manifest.

Here are some examples:

### PROSPERITY POT POURRI

Grind equal parts of cinnamon, nutmeg, poppy seeds and benzoin together, and combine with dried mint leaves and oats. Once ready, put in your office or under your bed.

### LOVE POT POURRI

Mix together rose petals, lavender and orange rind with a few drops of patchouli, sandalwood and jasmine oils. Fix with a teaspoon of orris root. Once ready, put beside your bed and in your underwear drawer.

### PROTECTION POT POURRI

Combine together a mixture of cloves, dill, rosemary, pepper and rue. Add benzoin as a fixer. Once ready, you can scatter it under your doormat or put it in a pot beside your front door.

There are many different kinds of pot pourri you can make. So experiment and allow your intuition to lead the way. It is also worth investing in a good magical herbal text – you will find a list of recommendations at the back of this book.

# The Magical Properties of Trees

Let's now have a look at the magical properties of trees. They are closely associated with woman's magic because of their affiliation with the thirteen pagan moon calendar.

## Trees associated with the thirteen pagan moons

| | |
|---|---|
| JANUARY | **Rowan** brings protection, healing and success. |
| FEBRUARY | **Ash** brings protection, prosperity and health. |
| MARCH | **Alder** brings healing and calm. |
| APRIL | **Willow** brings love, protection and healing. |
| MAY | **Hawthorn** brings fertility, happiness and chastity. |

JUNE
**Oak** brings strength, luck, love, potency, health and money.

JULY
**Hazel** brings luck, fertility, protection and wishes.

AUGUST
**Apple** brings love, healing and immortality.

SEPTEMBER
**Vine** brings strength, durability and prosperity.

OCTOBER
**Ivy** brings longevity and lucidity.

NOVEMBER
**Yew** brings everlasting life.

DECEMBER
**Mistletoe** brings protection, love, hunting, fertility and health.

BLUE MOON
This moon occurs every two to three years or so. Trees which carry properties of protection, exorcism, healing and purification such as **birch, elder, poplar** and **holly** are associated with this thirteenth moon.

## Other magical trees

Again, allow your own intuition to discover what other properties these trees possess for you. See if you can link with the guardian spirit of the tree, and allow yourself to be taken on an inner journey of discovery by it.

**Acacia** for protection

**Almond** for inner wisdom

**Apricot** to promote love

**Bamboo** for protection

**Broom** for purification and ardour

**Cedar** to instil strength and incorruptibility

**Chestnut** to draw prosperity and healing

**Cypress** for protection and healing

**Fir** to draw prosperity

**Lime** for healing and protection

**Mace** to raise psychic powers

**Maple** for love and abundance
**Mulberry** to protect against evil
**Myrtle** to draw love
**Olive** to find peace
**Palm** for fertility and to aid potency
**Peach** for making wishes come true
**Pear** for inducing lust as well as love
**Pine** to aid fertility and money matters
**Plum** for healing
**Quince** for growing happiness
**Walnut** to grant wishes and for strengthening the heart
**Witch hazel** induces charm and attractiveness

You can also use the magical qualities of your trees and plants to enhance the magic of your house. For instance, to draw love to your home, grow a myrtle tree on either side of the house, or ceremonially plant an apple tree where you can see it every day from the window. To protect your home from burglaries, grow two rosemary bushes either side of your front door. You can also grow a walnut tree, under which you can bury your desires in order to empower them. There are so many different ways of using the magic of plants and trees. Just enjoy the process.

In the next chapter we will look at the magical qualities of garden herbs, since they play such a key role in woman's magic and special occasions.

# Chapter 4
# Woman's Magic and Special Occasions

**W**E ARE HOW WE THINK, and we are what we eat. Combine thought and food together, and we enter into the heart of a woman's magic as well as into the core of the old religion.

Up until the industrial revolution, most people lived hand to mouth in rural areas. The land was their goddess because without its continued abundance, life ceased. This was a time when the balance between man and nature was at its most finite. The long, cold winters acted as a natural culling process since it was only the strongest who survived. Communities centred around farming with their calendar revolving around the four changes of season which were celebrated as the four great fire festivals: *Samhain* (31 October), the Festival of Apples, the food of the dead, and the night where the veil between the seen and unseen world is at its thinnest; *Imbolc* (2 February), the Festival of Light to celebrate the beginning of spring; *Beltaine* (30 April), the great fertility ritual; and *Lammas* (1 August), the Festival of Bread. These were celebrated with great reverence and respect even if they came to be conducted in secret out of fear of retribution from the church. Yet the great Christian festivals are all based on these ancient pagan farming rituals: *Samhain* became All Hallows' Eve or Hallowe'en; *Imbolc* became the church procession of Candlemas; *Beltaine* was virtually obliterated from the calendar since sexual expression was regarded as the work of the devil, and *Lammas*, the ancient Festival of Bread, became the Harvest Festival.

Preparation for these festivals was the natural domain of women, who would use special flowers, herbs and trees which resonated to particular magical qualities as table and room decorations. All the food served was, of course, seasonal, which added to the significance of the occasion; and according to the traditions of the old crafts, potentised and strengthened by spells, incantations and the direction in which the pot was stirred. The power of the sun was evoked by stirring clockwise, while the more subtle and feminine energies of the moon were summoned by stirring the pot anti-clockwise.

Yet, the most important ingredients were the blessings which were given to the food. Irrespective of religious practice, when this is done, it automatically raises the vibration of what is being eaten, as well as giving much needed thanks to the Goddess (or the Creator) for providing it. This brings us back to the importance of gratitude which we saw in Chapter 2. Unless we understand how to be grateful for what our world naturally supplies for us, we lose sight of ourselves as well as of the natural world which supports us.

This chapter, therefore, is about bringing the old crafts back into the kitchen of modern woman. It is about understanding that cooking is not a chore, but a holy act which creates magic in the lives of anyone we serve. It is also about becoming consciously aware of what nature provides for us, and how we can integrate the Goddess into our lives just by making something as simple as a piece of toast.

Just stop a minute and visualise this piece of toast, topped with butter and perhaps some marmalade. A tiny seed created the wheat to make your bread. A cow, somewhere, provided the milk to make your butter and oranges grew to make your marmalade.

All these ingredients rely on the abundance of the earth – and of the Goddess. **Everything you eat begins with the earth**. It's an awesome thought, is it not? And does she not deserve grateful thanks for providing it on a daily basis? Nature knew what she was doing when the world was created, and her intricate balance holds together the essence of earth power – without which life would not be sustained. This is why I believe it is totally sacrilegious for man to manufacture genetically modified food. By going against the will of nature, we are creating chaos of an unknown magnitude and nothing but harm will come from it – the consequences of which will be suffered by generations to come.

Woman's magic is about staying with the old ways, of practising reverence for what we are given, and for working with the preparation of food in a truly conscious way; even the most simple of dishes tastes of heaven when it has been prepared and cooked with love. Conscious cooking puts the magic back into the kitchen as well as into the stomachs of those we feed – and it is really fun to do because it means that we can also make any feast or celebration a really magical affair too.

## Buying and Preparing Food

Gone are the days of readily available organic products. Instead, supermarkets are stuffed with fruit and vegetables which have been force grown, sprayed with pesticides, shipped thousands of miles, pre-packed and irradiated – not to mention being passed through the dreaded barcode machine at the cash till. So, if you can, find a local organic supplier to buy your veggies from. The health benefits far outweigh the cost and effort.

Whatever you choose as your ingredients, make sure that you give blessings and thanks for them before beginning any food preparation. *This is particularly important if you are cooking meat.* The spirit of the animal needs to be honoured and blessed for sacrificing its life for your enjoyment. As your meal bubbles away, and as you stir the pot, keep sending it loving and healing thoughts. The difference in taste is quite remarkable.

You can use food magic for anything you want to create in your life; and there's no better place to start than a dash of love magic.

# A Romantic Evening for Two

The perfect evening to win your lover's heart through a spread of delights is a Friday, since that day is dedicated to the charms of Venus. Preferably it should fall in the waxing phase of the moon's cycle, especially if you are wanting to begin a relationship.

## Preparing the dining area

As well as paying homage to your guest, the decoration of the dining area is an important complement to any culinary feast. Making a love feast is especially wonderful to do for someone, so as you clean your dining area thoroughly, call on Aphrodite, Goddess of Love, to bring health and happiness to the person who comes to your table and to bless the relationship you are embarking upon.

### FLOWER DECORATIONS

Choose flowers which resonate to the energy of love such as jasmine, violets, roses and ivy, and place them in the direction of the south, since this inspires passion. You could also place an arrangement of camomile and lavender on the table which brings peace and harmony as well as honesty and integrity. If you want to seduce your intended, make sure you put red carnations in the room because these are said to contain very seductive fragrances!

If you do not have access to these flowers, make an arrangement of oranges, apples and nuts. These fruits also draw in love, and should be placed in the south.

You could also place a small arrangement of branches from one of the following trees over the door to draw special love blessings into the room:

> **Apple** to bind love
> **Apricot** to soothe the temperament
> **Cherry** to stimulate the emotions
> **Elm** to attract love
> **Lime** to promote love
> **Maple** to ensure longevity of love
> **Myrtle** to keep love alive
> **Willow** to gain insight about love

## ESSENTIAL OILS

To create a wonderfully erotic aroma, combine some oils from the list below. These oils have been used in love potions and as aphrodisiacs for centuries. Sprinkle a few drops on to the tablecloth, carpet and curtains to tantalise and seduce. Do remember, however, that aroma needs to be subtle. When it's too overpowering, it can have an adverse effect.

> **Cinnamon** to raise the vibration of love
> **Geranium** to protect love
> **Jasmine** to attract a higher spiritual love
> **Lavender** to sexually arouse a partner
> **Melissa** to quicken desire
> **Neroli** to attract a man
> **Patchouli** to induce passion
> **Rose** for pure love

**Sandalwood** to heal the heart
**Ylang-ylang** for seduction

## TABLE DECORATION

Red is the colour of passion; pink is the colour of romance; white is for purity; yellow for friendship; blue for healing communication; and green for opening the heart. So, depending on what you want to happen, choose your colours accordingly. For instance, if it is a night for seduction, use red or pink napkins and candles. If you want to build a friendship, but are not ready to step into a sexual union, choose blue, white or green. In the centre of your table float two red roses in a bowl of water with red or pink floating candles. According to legend, roses sprang from the blood of Adonis when he was killed by Ares out of jealousy because Ares's lover Aphrodite had fallen for his charms. Ever since then the rose has been symbolic of love and the ensign of Aphrodite, Goddess of Love.

You could also enhance the magic of your table by placing rose quartz crystals in your rose bowl or around its base.

## CANDLE MAGIC

You will need six red or pink candles. Place one in each of the four directions to create a sacred circle around the room and, as you do so, call on the devic guardians to provide a peaceful and loving atmosphere. Place the remaining two candles on the table. The magical significance of 2 brings peace and harmony while also summoning the power of moon magic. You can also anoint the candles with a few drops of your erotic oils which add to the potency of candle magic. As you light them, ask in your mind for love to flow freely between you and your lover.

## THE IDEAL FOOD FOR LOVE

An ideal feast for love needs to include such delicacies as shellfish, asparagus, luscious fruits and chocolates and, of course, plenty of bubbly to toast each other with. Do make sure that whatever you serve is not too heavy. After all, both of you may want to feel lithe and alert well into the small hours! The most important ingredients for your feast, however, are the herbs you use. These transform the simplest of dishes into potent aphrodisiacs, and you don't have to search any further than your kitchen cupboard for them either.

## Traditional love herbs

### BASIL (also known as witch's herb or St Joseph's wort): THE MOST POTENT LOVE HERB OF ALL

Basil originated in India where the Hindus consider it to be sacred. They dedicate it to Vishnu – the Hindu guide to the human soul whom, it is said, set the form of earth, air and heavens by taking three steps through the cosmos. Since basil vibrates to the energy of Mars, God of Lust, it is used prolifically in all sorts of love potions. Young girls from Crete rigorously encourage their basil plants to flourish because they believe that the plant draw their husbands to them. Should the plant wilt, so the plants will remain single. Basil is also used as a secret love message. Young lovers wear it behind their ears. When an admirer is allowed close enough to get a whiff, he knows his luck is in.

### CAMOMILE: TO SOOTHE THE HEART

This is the most soothing herb which is affiliated with the sun and the element of water. It has a wonderful folklore attached to it because it is said to remind us of humility: the more a camomile lawn is walked upon, the more it proliferates. It also brings peace of mind, so rather than pacing the floor in anticipation of the arrival of your lover you can either drink a cup of tea to steady your nerves or bathe in it. You can also scatter a few drops of the essential oil on to your bed sheet to raise passion.

### CLOVES: TO ATTRACT A LOVER
Cloves originate from trees which grow around the Indian Ocean and resonate to the planet Jupiter. A sprinkle of these in apple pie brings out their full flavour as well as their magical quality to attract a lover. You can also add cloves to mulled wine to give it a bit of an extra loving kick on a cold winter's night.

### CORIANDER: TO RAISE PASSION
A delicious peppery, spicy delight which resonates to the passionate energy of Mars and the element of fire. Coriander adds a taste of the exotic to any dish and it is said that when the seeds are added to a full-blooded red wine, it makes the most potent lust potion!

### DILL: TO MAKE YOURSELF IRRESISTIBLE
This gorgeous feathery herb originated in Asia and the warmer climates of Europe and vibrates to the energy of Mercury. It is reputed to make a person irresistible if they bathe in waters into which dill seeds have been thrown. Dill tea helps to stop hiccups, aids digestion and chewing the seeds will cure bad breath. Dill water also soothes a fretting baby as well as increasing the flow of breast milk.

### GINGER: A POTENT APHRODISIAC
Ginger resonates to the planet Mars and it is a very potent tropical aphrodisiac which induces the type of passion that can bring tears to the eyes of even the most ardent of lovers. You can use it to

perk up any dish, or even to make a hot spicy tea with a dash of lemon. Lemons are said to aid fidelity and to strengthen friendships. Ginger can also be added to a brew of Earl Grey tea to make it really different and completely delicious.

## MARJORAM (also known as oregano and wintersweet):
STRENGTHENS POTENCY

This highly evocative plant is associated with the planet Mercury. Its generic name is *origanum* which is derived from the Greek, literally meaning *joy of the mountains*. It is said to strengthen the potency of love when it is eaten in a meal. It was used in ancient times to help those who had died on their journey to the other side, and when found growing on a grave, it was said to be a symbol of the happiness of the dead one. Young married couples were also crowned with the herb to draw in blessings of love and fertility for their union.

## ROSEMARY: PROMOTES FERTILITY AND OPENS THE HEART

Rosemary resonates to the sun's energy so it is highly regarded as a powerful addition to any love potion. The 'dew of the sea' promotes fertility and love by opening the heart. However, should a man fail to be sensitive to its aroma, it is a sign that he is unable to love a woman fully. Nevertheless, when rosemary grows in profusion outside a house, it symbolises that the woman is very much the boss. Rosemary also cleans and purifies the atmosphere so if you need to talk matters through with your partner, place a drop or two of rosemary oil in a burner to aid the channels of communication.

## THYME: TO GATHER COURAGE

It is said that women who wear a sprig of thyme in their hair make themselves irresistible because it vibrates to the energy of Venus. There are two schools of thought on the origin of its name. The first comes from the Greek *thumus* which means *courage*. The second is from the Greek *thymia* meaning *to incite valour*. According to historians, maidens would embroider their handkerchiefs with thyme motifs and give them as talismans to their knights as they rode away to battle. So this is an important herb if you want to find the courage to speak the truth to your beloved, or indeed to propose marriage. Alternatively you could call upon its strengths when you need that extra piece of resolve to end a relationship. Drink a cup of thyme tea before your meeting and make sure you have a fresh sprig in your pocket. You could also burn it after your separation because this purifies the air of any negative thoughts.

## Fruit and vegetables of love

You can plan your menu around the following fruit and vegetables to draw in the kind of love experience you wish to manifest during the evening!

**Apples** to tempt love
**Asparagus** to fertilise love
**Avocados** to incite passion
**Bananas** to promote fertility
**Beetroot** to use as an ink for writing a love message
**Celery** to induce lust
**Figs** to spell-bind love
**Leeks** to bond love
**Lettuces** to prevent temptation
**Oranges** to ensure wedded bliss
**Peas** to bring fortune in love
**Plums** to heal love
**Quinces** to protect love
**Raspberries** to induce fertility and love

**Strawberries** to soothe the birth of a relationship

**Tomatoes** to raise passion

# Dining on Love with a Group of Friends

If you want to draw love into your life, you can create a special love feast with friends who are also wanting partners. Again, the best day to do this is on a Friday in the waxing phase of the moon. This could be a breakfast, lunch or supper gathering.

Ideally there should be six of you since 6 is the number of love. However, it doesn't really matter because it's more important to thoroughly enjoy yourselves. The ability to have fun is one of the most attractive qualities any of us possess, and a good belly laugh is probably the most powerful healing we can give to ourselves and to each other.

## What to bring

Each of your guests is required to bring a red rose and some food to share. The food needs to include such delicacies as tomatoes and avocados. Tomatoes originated in South America and were taken to Europe where they become known as Love Apples, while the avocado was regarded as an aphrodisiac by the Aztecs because it resembles certain parts of the male anatomy. Beans are also said to vibrate to love because of their macho shape! So perhaps you could make a hot spicy bean dish, pepped up by ginger, basil and coriander, and served with a side dish of avocado, Mexican style. As a dessert, you could create a wonderful fruit salad of love, and serve with it gorgeously thick double cream.

Whatever you decide to cook, have fun preparing

and making it together so you all imbue the food with lots of fun and laughter.

## The love ritual

You can perform this ritual before you begin to prepare the meal, or as it is cooking. Start your time together by ceremonially placing a pink candle in the four directions, and asking the guardian spirits and angels for help and support in making your dreams come true. Place the remaining two pink candles on the dining table. Each of you now needs to put your red rose into a vase. As this is done, you may want to say a few words about what type of relationship you want to manifest. Place this arrangement in the east – the direction which brings the new to fruition.

Now, take a few moments to write down what type of relationship each of you wants to create in your life. List what qualities you wish your partner to have, and do make sure you ask for someone who's free from other emotional ties. If you already have designs on someone **you must not ask for them by name**. In the old traditions this is regarded as black magic. It is highly dangerous to manipulate another person against their will, so just ask the universe to bring you someone who is for your highest good, and leave it at that.

As soon as you have all finished making your lists, take it in turns to read out what you have written. It is important to be witnessed and heard when you are creating magic for yourself. Place your lists in the area of the north, the direction of manifestation. You could create a little altar there if you wish. Once this has been done, you are now ready to dine in celebration knowing that the universe has received your heart's desire. Remember to give a toast of thanks to all your guides, ancestors and angels who will now be beavering away to create the right opportunities for your miracle of love to happen and for the right person to enter your life. This opens up a welcoming beam of light for them to follow straight to your heart. Enjoy your meal!

When it is time to go home, take your personal list with you, and keep it for three days and three nights in a safe and sacred place. You can then either burn it as an offering to Aphrodite, bury it in the ground under an apple tree, or tie a red ribbon around it, and put it away in a drawer on a sprig of lavender, where it will lie undisturbed.

Of course, it may take a little while before your partner materialises because they could be in the centre of the Amazon rain forest, or up a mountain in Tibet. On the other hand, they might just be in the shop next door, or at a dinner party you are about to be invited to. A friend of mine met his wife standing in a queue; another met her husband on a train. You can't tell how the universe is going to arrange it. But always bear in mind that when the time is right for your soul to grow through entering into a relationship, it doesn't matter where you are. You could be in a tent in the middle of the Sahara desert, and that special person will still come knocking on the flap!

The universe sometimes has a funny habit of sending out teasers when your love life is about to change. You can get a strange feeling that someone is on the way, or perhaps you suddenly feel compelled to do something, or go somewhere out of the ordinary – and bingo, there they are. Destined meetings always manifest precisely at the moment they are meant to, and this is something which no human can force, manipulate or conspire to create without the help and support of the universal consciousness.

# A Magical Wedding Feast

In the old days, the traditional time for 'hand-fasting' was performed by dancing around Beltaine fires on May Eve. Couples would join together for a year and a day, after which they could either re-commit to each other or go their separate ways. But, more importantly, this was the time when the May Queen and Stag performed a powerful sexual fertility rite to draw in the blessings of the Goddess for the whole community and the prosperity of the land. In celebration of the beginning of summer and the joy that it brought, people would decorate their houses with hawthorn flowers and wear it in their hair to draw in luck and fruitfulness. Although most of us have forgotten the sexual significance of May Day, the last remnants can be seen in the red and white maypole, and various Morris dances. So, if you want to make your wedding really magical, May is the perfect month to hold your nuptials.

Many people these days hold their wedding receptions in hotels or conference centres which lack heart and tend to give a 'corporate' look to the proceedings. If possible, do try and make it more magical and personal to you. You can do this by becoming consciously aware of the flowers that you use, choosing a menu which vibrates to love magic and by using colour combinations which resonate to the heart such as pink, red and green. Depending on the number of your guests, you can arrange tables to seat six, eight or twelve people each as 6 is the number of love, 8 draws in abundance and 12 is the number of cosmic order and perfection. Of course, if you love the old ways, you could also create little covens; tables of thirteen to represent the hidden magic of the Goddess herself!

## Table decoration

The strewing of rosemary sprigs on the floor around the wedding table is a wonderful gesture because as the bride and groom walk on it, its enchanting fragrance is released and opens the hearts of all present. Masses of hawthorn need to be put around the room too because of its fertility magic, together with myrtle which keeps love alive, rowan to bring luck and blessings, oak for sexual potency and willow for woman's magic. It is also said that when hawthorn, rowan and oak grow together, fairies appear!

Special love pot pourri can also be made from a combination of flowers traditionally used for weddings such as forget-me-nots for true love, rose buds for new love, lavender for the acknowledgement of love, violets for faithfulness and vervain for enchanting love. Add a fixative, together with six drops of geranium oil, and six drops of ylang-ylang oil. As you do so, call upon the blessing of the Goddess to be granted to the couple. The pot pourri needs to be divided into four bowls and placed in the four directions, accompanied by a pink candle. As the candles are lit at the start of the feast, the guardians of the four directions need to be acknowledged and paid homage to.

Traditionally, rice is thrown at the bride and groom since this guards against misfortune and also promotes fertility. However it is a beautiful gesture to strew fresh rose petals in their path instead. These not only produce a wonderful fragrance, but are also biodegradable, and therefore will probably be received more sympathetically by the vicar!

## THE BRIDE'S 'TUSSIE-MUSSIE'

'Tussie-mussies' were traditionally used to carry an array of special messages through the language of flowers. They

were especially popular in Victorian times, although during
Elizabethan times, and earlier, they were also made from
astringent herbs such as rosemary, thyme and rue which
acted as a disinfectant and protection against the plague,
and counteracted all manner of unsavoury street odours.

The bride's tussie-mussie is a very important addition
to her wedding regalia. A really magical combination of
flowers is ivy for fidelity, pink roses for romantic love,
myrtle for longevity, and sage to attract wisdom and
protection and to grant wishes. Of course there are many
other combinations of flowers and herbs which can be
used, but do be aware that whatever magic you take to the
altar with you, you will carry into your married life. The
tussie-mussie needs to be placed on the wedding table as
part of the floral decoration because the bride and groom
'consume' its magical qualities as they enjoy their feast.

## The feast preparations

Most people arrange for outside caterers to provide the
wedding feast. If this is your decision, do ask for a dish to
be decorated with fresh herbs such as basil, coriander and
dill. These will automatically imbue the feast with love
magic. You will also need to bless the spirit of any meat
which is being served. This animal has died to bring you joy.
Make sure the dessert includes oranges and strawberries if
possible since oranges bring wedded bliss and strawberries
smooth the path of love.

For those of you who want a more personal
approach, the most wonderful place to conduct a wedding
is outside in nature under an apple tree, where you say
your own vows to each other, surrounded by a loving
sacred circle of friends. Afterwards, you can leap the flames
of the marriage fire together and jump the besom to

symbolise your commitment to each other. Jumping the besom is a pagan tradition where a broom is laid on the floor and the couple leap over it. You can also entrust the feast preparations to a friend who will make sure that each morsel will be full of blessings from the Goddess and filled with love and good wishes. Each platter can be decorated with flower heads such as pansies which symbolise loving thoughts, or jasmine which represents spiritual union.

# A Feast for Letting Go of the Old, and Welcoming in the New

This is a wonderful thing to do when you feel that you are ready to free yourself from the emotional entanglement of an old relationship, and are willing to move into a new life.

Send out special invitations to your dearest friends to share in this celebration and ask them to bring food offerings which you can all prepare together. Ideally you need to choose a day during the waning phase of the moon since this is the time for releasing old thoughts and patterns.

 ## Cleansing your home of the old

Since this is a very powerful statement you are making for yourself, it is a good idea to completely clear out all your unwanted bits and pieces as a prelude to your feast. Clean the house thoroughly too, and buy new bed linen. In fact replace anything which causes you to hang on to the past. You could use a switch made from birch twigs. Birch was traditionally used to cleanse negativity out of rooms by beating the air. Alternatively you could use a traditional 'witch's broom' to sweep the area. These wonderful 'besoms' are made from a combination of woods: ash is used for the shaft which symbolises the male principle, rebirth, healing and protection; the brush is made from birch twigs for their cleansing and purification qualities as well as representing the feminine. This is bound by the willow which brings love, protection, and healing. It is also the tree affiliated to the moon, and therefore woman's magic. Burning a sage stick is another way of clearing out old memories and purifying the atmosphere.

## FLOWERS

Decorate the house with flowers such as camomile to bring peace and harmony, lily of the valley to symbolise a return to happiness, pyrethrums to symbolise forgiveness, irises to bring faith and wisdom, and orchids to behold beauty in your future. Carnations can also be used since they represent pure love.

## DECORATING THE TABLE

Since this is a time for healing your heart, decorate the table with green and blue china, napkins and candles. Place a special bowl of pot pourri in the room, made from rose petals and lavender which bring healing to your heart, and place a vase of chrysanthemums on the table. This symbolises your willingness to let go of any bad feelings you have had towards your ex-lover.

## PREPARING THE FOOD

Make this a really special occasion by treating yourself to your favourite dishes – together with what you love to drink. Allow your friends to help you too. This will remind you that your future is full of loving people who have your best interests at heart. Empower your feast with blessings from the Goddess, and ask for it to be imbued with the qualities of wisdom and resolve. There is to be no going back to a relationship which fails to serve you in your full glory as a remarkable woman.

During your meal, make time to pay homage to your ex-partner by thanking them for all the lessons you have learnt from your time together. Wish them well with their future life and loves, and invite your guests to raise a glass to toast them. And now it is time to toast all the new doors which will start opening to you now you have set your heart free.

The following day, you can bury a small offering of food from your feast under a favourite tree as you give thanks to the Goddess and ask her to bless your new life.

# Feasting on Abundance

The best evening to conduct a feast of abundance is on a Thursday, the day of Jupiter – planet of expansion and benevolence, during the waxing phase of the moon.

Monday is also relevant since this is the day of the moon, and its silver colour resonates to the vibration of money. However, it doesn't really matter because abundance and prosperity can arrive in many ways and on any day. The most important thing is that you are conscious of what you are creating and are always respectful of the magic you are weaving.

## Herbs associated with drawing in abundance and prosperity

**ALLSPICE:** ATTRACTS MONEY AND LUCK
This delicate plant resonates to the planet Mars and is traditionally used in prosperity spells by burning it on a charcoal block placed on an altar.

**BASIL:** ATTRACTS WEALTH

Basil is a truly magical plant because not only does it draw in love, it also possesses strong powers to attract wealth. The Hindus place sprigs of it in each room of their house to attract prosperity and for protection.

**BAY LEAVES:** TO REALISE AMBITION, FAME AND FORTUNE

Bay is affiliated to the planetary forces of Mercury. In ancient times a wreath of bay leaves was used to crown poets and heroes, sportsmen and great statesmen. This can be traced back to the mythological tale of Apollo and Daphne. Apollo relentlessly pursued Daphne against her wishes. To escape him, she begged the gods to change her into a laurel bush. Apollo immediately declared the tree as sacred and from then on, in Daphne's honour, he wore a wreath of laurels around his head. He also commanded all those returning from victory to do the same. Thus the bay became associated with fame, glory and public recognition. Poets are associated with the bay because it is said to clear the head and aid concentration. You can also put a few fresh leaves into your drawer at work to realise your career ambitions.

**CINNAMON:** PROMOTES SUCCESS

Cinnamon resonates to the sun, comes from the Far East and was used in ancient religious rituals which date back to the Egyptian dynasty. God commanded Moses to incorporate it into a holy oil to be used for sacred anointment purposes and the Romans used the leaves to create wreaths which were hung in their temples to heighten spiritual powers. It can be burnt on a charcoal block to attract success or used as an oil to anoint green candles to draw prosperity.

**CLOVES:** ATTRACT RICHES

Cloves are used to attract financial wealth and to drive away any negative forces. Therefore if you want to draw money to you, keep a few cloves in your pocket as you go about your daily business.

## MINT: DRAWS IN MONEY AND COOLS NEGOTIATIONS

Persephone turned the beautiful nymph Minthe into a plant out of jealousy when she saw that her lover, Pluto, had fallen in love with her. In retaliation, Pluto cast a remembrance spell on his beloved so that the more that mint is walked upon, the sweeter its scent becomes. Mint is governed by Mercury and its tendency to spread rampantly symbolises its ability to attract wealth and prosperity. The word *mint* comes from the Latin *mens* meaning *mind*, because it also has the power to strengthen the mind and fortify intelligence. It is therefore very useful to drink before a difficult business meeting, and it is advisable to serve mint tea if it appears that tempers are beginning to fray.

## NUTMEG: INCREASES PROSPERITY

This lovely earthy nut vibrates to the energy of the planet Jupiter. Its brown appearance reminds us of the fertility of the earth, and is therefore used in prosperity spells by sprinkling it on to pieces of charcoal or into the flames of green candles.

## Vegetables and fruits of abundance

**Bananas** increase fertility and cure impotency
**Blackberries** represent an abundance of prosperity
**Grapes** raise potency and increase fertility
**Onions** to draw money
**Oranges** are a symbol of luck and good fortune
**Peas** – shelling peas brings good fortune
**Pineapples** – the flesh attracts money

**Pomegranates** – the seeds represent abundance and money luck

**Rice** represents abundance of money

**Tomatoes** bring prosperity

## What to bring

Eight is the number of prosperity and abundance, so you could invite eight guests. Again, it doesn't really matter about this; the important thing is to invite those who are willing to enter into the spirit of it all. It is important that everyone contributes to the feast with food as well as wine. Make sure that you all dress up to greet your abundance. Cover yourselves in diamante, or diamonds for that matter, and wear the most expensive clothes you possess. The universal law says like attracts like, so make sure you reflect exactly what you want!

Ask each of your guests to bring a small gift which is given at some point like a lucky dip. This represents the ethos of *'as you give, so you receive'*. They also need to bring a personal symbol of prosperity which they can put on a special altar placed in the direction of the north, the area of manifestation. On the altar there should be two green candles and a huge bowl overflowing with succulent fruit and nuts.

## Decorating the dining area

Green is the traditional colour of prosperity, but you can also use gold, silver, orange and yellow. Make your table looks as if it is groaning with abundance, and arrange vases full of flowers such as periwinkle, honesty, honeysuckle, poppies and fresh mint around the room. If you are doing this in winter, use holly and ivy to represent the evergreen of eternal life. You could also use a jasmine plant. Put two candles in each of the four directions, totalling eight in all, and place an arrangement made from the leaves and branches of one of the following trees:

**Ash** – burn on a yule log to draw prosperity
**Cedar** to draw in money
**Elder** to ensure prosperity
**Maple** for lasting abundance
**Myrtle** to increase fertility
**Oak** 'out of little acorns . . .'
**Poplar** to attract money

Make an evocative fragrance out of eight drops of any of the following oils in water and scatter over the carpets and curtains or put into an oil burner:

**Basil** for attracting wealth
**Bergamot** for earthing wealth
**Cinnamon** to attract success
**Jasmine** to draw wealth
**Mint** for attracting money
**Nutmeg** to expand prosperity
**Patchouli** to enhance fertility
**Pine** to attract abundance

## The ritual

As each of your guests arrive, present them with a cup of warmed, rich red wine to which a pinch of cinnamon, nutmeg and orange peel has been added. These spices attract riches. Pre-dinner nibbles could include grapes with cubes of pineapple on sticks. Both are well-known additives to money spells. Almonds, cashew nuts and pecan nuts also resonate to wealth, so make sure there are several dishes overflowing with them.

When you feel ready, gather everyone together to ceremonially light the candles, and call upon the guardian devas, your angels and spirit guides to bless your evening. It is now time to write down exactly what you all want to manifest in your lives. Once this has been completed, sit together in a circle and take it in turns to share your wishes. Join hands for a few moments to really empower the wish before moving on to the next person. When you have all spoken your truth, sprinkle your lists with a few drops of patchouli oil and place them on your prosperity altar in the direction of the north. And now for the feast!

Start by each guest in turn giving gratitude to the earth for providing such wonders. You can also enjoy your lucky dip gift. At the conclusion of your meal, each person takes home their wish list which they keep for a whole cycle of the moon. After this it can be burnt or buried in homage to the Goddess.

Make a note of how your prosperity begins to change. It may come through strange coincidences which lead you to a better-paid job, or some money may fall into your lap out of the blue. Share your miracles with each other regularly and, if you so desire, make a feast of abundance a regular occurrence, just for the pure joy of it.

## Putting the Magic Back into Christmas

Before Christmas was celebrated there were magnificent ancient yule celebrations in which great logs were burnt on ritual fires to symbolise the return of the sun god Sol and the beginning of longer daylight hours. *Yule* is a Nordic word meaning *wheel*, which symbolised the divine spiral of never-ending life. This celebration occurred on the winter solstice, which was also the day that chief Druids would cut the sacred mistletoe from the boughs of apple trees, and on rare occasions when it was found, from their beloved oaks. It was believed, when this happened, that the mistletoe would possess unique healing powers as well as magical strength.

The date of 25 December was revered as a special day because it was heralded as the great sun god Sol's birthday. In an effort to stamp out these hoary pagan customs, the Christian fathers adopted 25 December as Jesus's birthday and, over time, the winter solstice customs became lost in Christian myth. However some semblance of the old traditions remain through the Christmas feast, and the use of holly, ivy and mistletoe as decoration in our homes. Evergreen was brought into the house to act as a reminder that life would return, even though death was all around in nature. The holly represented the male aspect with its vibrantly sexual red berries, and the ivy, the more gentle, feminine principle. Because of its countless curative and magical properties, mistletoe was the Druids' most revered plant, and people would take it into their homes as a talisman for protection, fertility, health and, of course, love.

These days, for most of us, the heart has gone out of Christmas. It has been replaced by ferocious marketing campaigns which persuade us to buy presents we can't really afford and which the recipient doesn't really need, let alone want. We drag ourselves to church out of duty and then spend the rest of the day glued to the television, or having emotional negotiations with relatives who have outstayed their welcome. To put the magic back where it belongs, we need to reintroduce the old rituals of paying homage to the return of the sun on the winter solstice. We also need to realise that the symbology of Christ's birth is, once again, based on the old ways.

The winter solstice has always been associated with the miraculous birth of a baby. This is not actually a baby, but the representation of the birth of the new year and therefore a time of innocence. The births of Dionysus or Bacchus, Lord of Fecundity, Mithras, the Roman god associated with the ancient bull cult, and Baal, the Syrian fertility and storm god which infiltrated European culture through the Roman empire, were also celebrated at this time. In Christian mythology, Jesus represents the 'new baby', while Mary symbolises innocence.

In the old traditions, the winter solstice or 25 December was a time when people would build a shrine to the Holly King, or Herne, Lord of the Forest, who promised to provide through the winter. It was also a time to pay respect to the grief of Demeter who is steeped in mourning the loss of her daughter Persephone to Hades, Lord of the Underworld. Yet this time also symbolised new hope as the season turned towards spring. Your feast, therefore, needs to be truly abundant, with the table and room decked with masses of holly and ivy, and with plenty of yellow or red candles to signify the power of Sol's return. It is also a lovely gesture to set a place at the table for the 'absent ones' – these are your ancestors, guides and angels who nurtured you from the unseen realms.

## A winter solstice ritual

You can conduct a lovely ritual to take you into the new year. This is a fire ceremony which you can do together as a family, with a group of friends, or by yourself.

Light a red candle to Sol, and write down everything which no longer serves you in your life. Once you have completed this, close your eyes and call out for the Goddess to appear in your mind's eye. Give her everything you wrote on your list, and watch her change them into fertiliser for your soul. Now open your eyes, and burn your list in the flame of the candle.

Next, write down everything you want to give birth to from a place of innocence in the coming year. When you are ready, close your eyes and call for the Goddess to appear. Tell her what you want to create for yourself, and watch the seeds of these new wishes growing out of the fertiliser she made for you. The Goddess also bears a gift of insight for you for the coming year. Allow her to place it into your heart – when the time is right, this gift will be revealed to you. Give thanks to the Goddess and, when you are ready, open your eyes. Keep your wish list in a safe place, or on your altar, so you can remind yourself of what you are aiming for throughout the year.

## Putting the Magic into any Festive Occasion

You can make any festive occasion magical just by lighting candles and performing a simple ritual to ask for the blessings of the Goddess. If you want to pursue conscious cooking, then do invest in a few specialist magical books. I have recommended some in the bibliography section. If this sounds too complicated, the main thing to remember is to infuse your cooking with loving thoughts, and to decorate the table and room with flowers and colours which resonate to the magic you want to create. This act alone will change even the most reluctant cooks' approach to kitchen chores!

# Chapter 5
# Woman's Magic in Spirals and Cycles

IN THIS CHAPTER, WE ARE going to look at how unseen cosmic forces influence our lives, and bring opportunities for our spiritual awareness to develop as women. Women are particularly sensitive to these forces because we naturally enact the great cycle of life every month through menstruation, while also carrying the light of creation within our bodies. When I began to open up to the concept that these forces actually lived inside me I felt an incredible sense of awe and reverence for life. Something – call it God, Buddha, the Creator, or whatever you wish – has provided us with more majesty and mystery than anyone could possibly dream of.

The sadness is that so many women have forgotten that we are all part of this magnificent creation, and each one of us has a totally unique relationship with it. However, those of the ancient world certainly knew, and searched for ways of working with it rather than attempting to conquer it. They also realised that everything in the heavens was a reflection of our behaviour on earth, and that all life was governed by cycles and spirals. So the 'round art' of astrology was born alongside the mystical use of numbers which provides us with a sort of pragmatic explanation of how these energies work within us as great life cycles. Before we delve into how these life cycles form in astrological terms and have a bit

of fun working out which numerological cycle we fall into, I want
to say a little more about cosmic forces and our spiral of consciousness.

## The Cosmic Forces

The cosmic forces make up 'the way' of who we are as 'hu-man'
beings and how our lives automatically fall into the cycles which
influence the natural world. Indeed, *hu* is derived from the Latin
*humus* meaning *creature of the earth*. *Hu* is also a sound vibration or
chant used by the Buddhists, Sufis and other Eastern religions to
open the heart to the innate and endless flow of universal love.
'The way' refers to the teachings of the *Tao* which have been
embraced and practised for over 6,000 years by all of the great
sages, mystics and teachers.

The concept of *as above, so below* has been adopted by man
since the earliest time. The circular celestial sphere in which our
universe is contained can be seen in the magnificent cycles of
nature on earth and in the extraordinary patterns of all living
things, from rings in the bark of trees and the migratory habits of
birds to the cylindrical shapes of tornadoes and the rhythmical
tides of our rivers and oceans. It is also perfectly reflected by the
innermost workings of human physiology. The miraculous orbit
of minuscule atoms around their nuclei, which gives us our spark
of life, echoes the movement of the world as it orbits its own
nucleus, the sun. Incidentally, the word *world* comes from the
Anglo Saxon *weoruld* meaning *course of man's life*.

## The Spiral of Consciousness

Everything comes full circle before it can move to a higher level
of consciousness. This concept is enacted right through the
universe, from the earth and planets transiting through the

zodiac belt to the cycles of nature on earth. As each cycle of existence is completed, another automatically begins at a slightly different or higher vibration – and so the spiral continues. For example, as each year concludes, another starts, yet it cannot retrace the steps of the old; it has to move forward on to a different vibration on the spiral for progress to continue.

This spiral activity of the physical world is echoed deep within our own psyches, driving us forward to find our true potential. As humans, with the gift of free choice, we can make a conscious decision to either aim for a personal higher state of being, or continue along a well-trodden path. I believe that human consciousness is a spiral directly linked to karmic patterns which we need to break through to move forward on our spiritual path. Research suggests that human spirals are constructed from many layers of energy circuits, each resonating to a particular emotional vibration. Each circuit provides an opportunity for growth and expansion to take place within our consciousness. It attracts its own likeness through similar thought patterns, lifestyles and people who are resonating at the same level. If a particular life lesson is not fully absorbed at that level, around we go again until we have completely grasped it and broken the emotional energy circuit within us.

I can remember years ago being incredibly unhappy in a job. My boss was foul-mouthed and unkind. I desperately wanted to change my life, but rather than take time out to consider what was happening to me, and what I really wanted to do, I jumped ship straight into another, very similar job. My new boss turned out to be just as foul mouthed and rude, and a friend of the old one to boot! Looking back, I realised that although I had changed my job, I hadn't changed me inside. I had just remained on the same low self-worth energy circuit, transferring all my desperation and personal unhappiness from one working situation to another.

# WOMAN'S MAGIC IN SPIRALS AND CYCLES

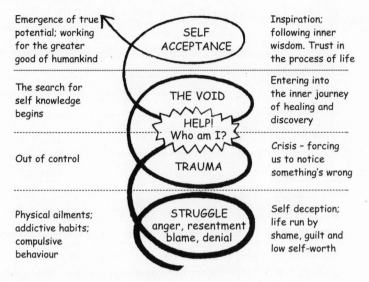

Emergence of true potential; working for the greater good of humankind

SELF ACCEPTANCE

Inspiration; following inner wisdom. Trust in the process of life

The search for self knowledge begins

THE VOID

HELP! Who am I?

Entering into the inner journey of healing and discovery

Out of control

TRAUMA

Crisis – forcing us to notice something's wrong

Physical ailments; addictive habits; compulsive behaviour

STRUGGLE anger, resentment blame, denial

Self deception; life run by shame, guilt and low self-worth

Once we realise that we are responsible for what we create in our lives, we are ready to pass on to a higher state (or spiral) of understanding. Our learning however, does not cease. Each level of the spiral contains a new set of lessons which we need to learn. Thus we continue to evolve right to the end of our lives.

Since every one of us directly carries the energy of the universe within us, it would follow that as each of us attain a higher state of being, this affects the entire spiritual evolution of the world at large. Therefore we, as individuals, are personally responsible for what the whole of humanity creates. Looking at how we behave towards each other across the world can be pretty depressing. However, I believe that as more and more of us embrace a consciously loving way of life, which is respectful of our environment as well as each other, the entire consciousness of humanity will begin to shift in a positive way as well. So, your commitment to yourself as a woman and to your spiritual development is vital to the way in which our world is to progress into the next century.

## Ritual for travelling the spiral within

By working with your inner spiral of consciousness, you can begin to understand your own evolutionary process, what lessons you are currently facing, what you have already overcome and where you are heading. You will need paper and coloured pens for this ritual, so make sure they are beside you after you have completed a short relaxation and inner visualisation exercise. You could also make your own tape recording of this ritual visualisation to act as an audio guide.

Create a quiet ambience, somewhere you will not be disturbed for at least an hour. Light a candle for yourself and your inner wisdom, together with some incense or an essential oil burner. Take three deep breaths and slowly begin to relax into who you really are. Notice any feelings which may arise – how you are feeling about yourself, or any worries which may be consuming your mind and preventing you from fully entering into this process. Just allow them to be, and then gently but firmly release them as you breathe out. Allow your body to sink further into the chair or floor cushion and, when you are ready, close your eyes. Ask for your higher wisdom to appear in the form of a guide. Notice that this guide offers you a gift of insight which is to help you understand your experience more fully. Your guide will now escort you into your inner spiral of consciousness. See or feel it clearly surrounding you. What does it look like? What colour is it, and what message is it carrying? Take time to absorb its significance and, when you feel ready, begin to notice what you need to do for yourself to be able to move further into your spiral of life. Do you have emotional problems which are causing stagnation in your life, or are you afraid of stepping into your true power and potential as a woman? If so, you can now journey back, with the help of your guide, through your spiral into your past to cut any etheric ties with family members or people who may have caused you humiliation, embarrassment, pain or fear. Invite them to stand before you and, as they do so, place your hand on their hearts, and allow them to place their hand on your heart. Feel the energy flowing between you, and allow any negative feelings to float out of your body. Stay with this vision until you are able to release yourself from any guilt, hurt or blame associated with this person. As you do this, you may begin to feel physical sensations in your body. Take particular notice if you are feeling these sensations in your breasts, womb or sexual centre and breathe out any blockages.

Once you feel complete, pay homage to this person for the lessons they brought into your life, then bid them farewell. See the etheric ties between you dissolve and know that your karmic relationship with them is now complete. It is time to move on. As you free yourself, you may well begin to experience a feeling that you are touching a depth of your femininity you have never felt before; that a sense of power is beginning to pervade your entire being. This is the light of the Goddess beginning to shine upon you.

As soon as you feel complete, return to your present life spiral, and notice if anything has changed around you. If there is a shift, no matter how subtle, you can be sure that changes will begin to manifest in your daily life too. Once you feel ready, say farewell to your guide, and know that at any time you can return to your inner spiral of consciousness to find insight, wisdom and guidance.

When you feel ready, write a full account of your experience and of all the people whom you have released. You can also draw a picture or diagram of your spiral and instinctively place yourself somewhere upon it. This can show you how far you have come in your evolution, and where you are heading.

I had a very powerful experience during one of my own spiral visualisations. I realised that I was being held back by a thick black cord which was attached to someone from my past. This black cord was full of venom and hatred. So I travelled down my spiral to meet with them. As soon as I stood before them in my mind's eye, I clearly saw that they had come into my life to teach me about the misuse of sexual power. I immediately thanked them for the lesson, and then asked for their forgiveness for any hurt I had caused them, while granting my own total absolution. The black cord seemed to disintegrate, and instantly I felt the whole of the left side of my body (traditionally associated with femininity) fill up with light, from the tips of my toes to the top of my head. It was quite an extraordinary sensation because suddenly I felt like a 'full' woman for the first time. Although I was completely unaware of it, it was as if I had been walking around half empty. Many things began to change in my life after that, especially how I felt about myself in relationships.

Using creative techniques like this brings your inner visions into reality and provides you with a practical record to which you can refer when events in your daily life become challenging or confusing. Then, when the darkness does indeed creep up upon you, just remember that you are your own source of wisdom, love and light, and this will help you to find the way ahead once more.

## Using the spiral to explore past lives

By allowing yourself to travel down through your spiral you can also take yourself beyond your conception, back into past lives.

Following the relaxation techniques, meet with your guide and then allow yourself to travel back down the spiral of your life to your birth. Notice how you feel at this juncture, and if your birth was easy or difficult. What was your mother feeling as she gave birth to you? See what instinctively comes to mind and, if necessary, write your experience down.

Now take yourself into the womb. Feel your mother's heart beating, and her warm body protecting you. Move further and further back until you find yourself at the point of your conception. Why did you choose these two people, from the billions of others on the planet, to create life for you, and why was incarnating into this particular family dynamic so important for your personal growth? Allow yourself time to write down any insights you may have.

Now take yourself beyond your conception into the great void, and call out for your past life spirals to appear before you. How many of them are there? Are there some which appear to be greater lifetimes than others and what messages do they carry? You can also see if you can discover how many lifetimes you have chosen to take on the mantle of the Goddess by becoming a woman, and how this influences your present life.

I discovered that I have had many more lifetimes as a woman than a man, and during this life, I have carried over much of my inherent esoteric and occult knowledge from several past lives as a priestess and teacher. The more I open up to this ancient knowledge, the more I feel comfortable with who I really am.

Just trust your inner vision, and the loving support of your guide. It may be appropriate to enter into a particular past life spiral to see if you are indeed carrying anything from it into your current life. Perhaps there is unfinished business to attend to which is manifesting through people who presently surround you. Allow your imagination to release what has lain dormant in your subconscious. Whether you believe in past lives or not, by allowing your inner wisdom to speak a truth, albeit disguised as a past life experience, you can feel the effects of this truth vibrating in your soul. So be generous and patient with yourself, and enjoy playing with it.

Once you feel complete, allow your guide to escort you back through your conception, through the moment of your birth, to your present age. Pay homage to your guide and, when you feel ready, write down your experience.

## Using the spiral to explore your potential

Since you can go down the spiral of consciousness, you can also move forward through it to explore your potential as a woman. Again, allow yourself to relax, and call upon the support and help of your guide.

As you look forward, see a beautiful light calling to you in the distance. This is the light of your true potential as a woman on earth. When you feel ready, begin to walk towards this light. As you pass through the spiral notice when the colours change, or if new feelings or visions arise. These mark important times to come, so make a note of them. As you reach the light, you see a magnificent woman standing with arms open to receive you. This magnificent woman holds the key to help you pass into the next level of your spiral, so allow yourself to receive her wisdom either as a vision or a feeling.

Now step into her arms, and allow yourself to surrender into the manifestation of your own ultimate feminine. What does this feel like? Take time to absorb her into your heart and notice if this is affecting any part of your body. Breathe out any blockages which are preventing her from fully entering your inner being.

Once you feel complete with her, stand before her and make a vow that you will honour her by being her living embodiment on earth. This means treading the path of truth and integrity, and shining her light of love wherever you go.

You can now return down the spiral until you find yourself back in your present life cycle. Notice if anything has changed since you embarked on this inner journey, and how you are feeling about yourself as woman who has experienced her true power and potential. Pay homage to your guide and, when you are ready, write down your experience.

## Using the spiral to help release addictions

Any kind of addiction is a cry for help in some way. In reality, addictive behaviour is a cover for the pain that our soul is suffering. We stuff ourselves with food, alcohol, tobacco, drugs or anything which will numb us for just that little bit longer. Nevertheless, these addictions increase our low self-worth and self-hate because, no matter what we do to our bodies, our pain will remain steadfast until we take responsibility for it.

If you are suffering from an addiction which you desperately wish to break, conducting the following ritual will help you to release yourself from it.

Light a white candle for yourself and a blue one for your addiction. Blue is the colour of healing. If appropriate you can burn some incense as well. Close your eyes and ask your guide to appear in your mind's eye. Allow your

guide to take you into your spiral of consciousness and see
your addictive habits before you. Let these habits grow
into huge indulgences. For example, a vast mountain of
food, or thousands of cartons of cigarettes, piles of drugs,
hundreds of bottles of drink, or whatever you use as an
addiction. Really see it and relish it, make your mouth
water with it, and then pile in and stuff yourself until you
are sick of it.

When you have reached this point, step back from
your addictions, and see a black cord which comes from
your past attached to a certain part of your body.
Accompanied by your guide, follow the cord back into
your past until you find the point – or age – when this
addiction began. See who was around you, and what
circumstances created this pain inside you. It is time now to
forgive and to release yourself from the cause. Ask your
guide to help you melt away the addictive cord, and to pull
its roots out of your body. It is time to leave it behind.
Once you feel complete, you can return with your guide
to where you indulged your habit. See how you are feeling
inside, and watch your reaction when faced with your
addiction again. Step into the middle of it, and then ask for
the light from your future potential as a woman, free of
these addictions, to shine its loving light on you.
Surrender yourself to this light, and watch it melt away
your habitual desires from around you. Allow yourself to
be washed clean and, as you experience this, open your
heart up to release the pain which you have been hiding all
these years. Breathe the pain out of your body and, if
necessary, hold something soft like a pillow to your heart as
a comfort. Once you feel complete, give thanks to the
light, and to your guide, and open your eyes.

Write down everything you have experienced, and

any insights you may have gained. You can also draw your experience, and allow your inner wisdom to provide you with more clues about how these addictions came about.

You can use this visualisation as many times as you wish to help you to break the power of your destructive habits. You can also adapt it to help you release emotional obsessions such as self-hate, lack of confidence, sexual addiction and so on. Just make sure that you create a sacred environment before you begin, and pay homage to yourself by lighting a candle. When you conclude your visualisation, remember to give thanks for the support of your guide and to your higher self.

# Entering into the Higher Spiral

We know when we have broken the mould of past hurts which kept us chained to base negative reactions because we suddenly realise that we are no longer victims of what life throws at us, or indeed of other people's negative behaviour or opinions. Instead, we willingly surrender ourselves to a magical flow which seems to carry us along all by itself. Usually, however, before we pass through to the higher levels of our spiral, it may seem as if we have to pass a massive test of courage, strength and will to carry on in the face of adversity. It is as if the Goddess is testing our worthiness to become her representative on earth.

This often manifests as a dark night of the soul, a time when everything seems to fall away, leaving us feeling as if we have been stripped naked and left out in the cold to perish alone and lost. Although this is a terrible place to find ourselves, it is nevertheless a great initiation. My own initiation involved my partner leaving me for another woman, my beloved cat dying and losing my home. Yet even though my life had been wrecked virtually overnight, I knew deep inside that something much greater was coming for me. I had no other choice but to completely surrender myself into the arms of the Goddess because I knew she was calling me to her. And I was right! Within a relatively short space of time, I moved somewhere I had always wanted to live, and everything began to slot into place to provide me with a much more solid and nurturing way of life, and my work took on a new meaning. Looking back on those events, I now realise that I was ready to make the great leap of faith, and just needed a good shove to do it.

## Honouring the state of transition

Any life change, whether it is foisted on to us or not, needs time for the dust to settle before it can really move us into a new way of being. We have to go through a period of transition for our energies to transmute from one level of being to another. It is as if we are increasing our electrical wattage. Every time this happens to me, I end up blowing all the lights at home, or my car breaks down in some way. A friend of mine blew the fuses on her hairdryer, washing machine, fridge and telephone all in one week while she was undergoing some deeply cathartic therapy! So take note if electrical appliances in your home are synchronistically breaking down as you go through a time of transition.

In nature, spring follows winter; night follows day. This is the natural way of all things, and shows why we also need times of darkness or inactivity before we can begin a new life for ourselves. We should learn to honour these times and take the opportunity to understand why things are dying out of our life instead of becoming depressed because these fallow times are lonely and frightening. By learning to embrace and trust the natural cycle of life and death which is also programmed into our own psyches, we can learn to wait patiently for the sun to shine again and use this time well to plan a much more productive and worthy life.

With this wholeness comes simplicity because, as we finally surrender to our destiny, our life's mission also begins to emerge. This is accompanied by a sense of peace and acceptance that we are indeed on this earth for a higher purpose which is enhanced by being a woman. We begin to love what we do and do what we love, and there is no separation between our private and working lives. Our personal and sexual integrity is paramount and we hold ourselves proudly as wise women who know that we make a valuable contribution to society.

Discovering our life's path does not mean that we need to become banner-wavers for the 'new age' either. It could be that we are ready to draw to us a partner who also possesses a higher sense of spiritual awareness with whom we wish to create a family. Alternatively, we may be embarking on a new business venture which is geared towards helping others to become more aware of themselves and their environment in some way. Whatever it is, it is done in the full knowledge that we are part of the universal flow of light and love, and we are willing to take full responsibility for ourselves as spiritually evolved women.

## Planetary Life Cycles

It is now time to take a look at the wonders of those heavenly wanderers, the planets, and the part they play at pertinent times in our lives.

The word *crisis* comes from the Greek *to discern* or *to judge*. Our life's path is full of experiences which make us pay attention to what is happening to or around us, and it is by experiencing crisis that we can learn to understand what works for us and what does not. However, it would also appear that these crises are more prevalent at certain ages, for example, the infamous mid-life crisis which happens around the age of forty-two. Astrologers say that these crises are brought about by the transits of the five outer planets of Jupiter, Saturn, Uranus, Neptune and Pluto which ignite certain energy patterns within us as they travel around the circle of our astrological chart. These ignitions occur when the five planets make an aspect to their own natal placements:

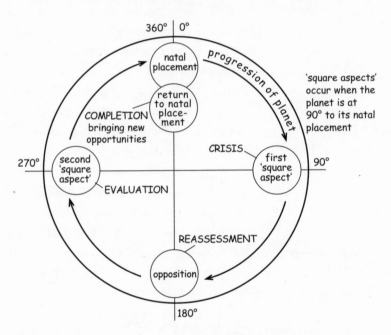

Due to their constant circular motion, the planets provide us with a chance to face certain issues more than once in a life-time, as well as offering us an opportunity to start again as they 'return' to their original natal placement. Thus by learning from our mistakes we can grab the opportunity to put things right where they may well have gone awry, and begin the new cycle with a far clearer idea of who we really are and what we want to achieve.

The following planetary movements are based on approxi-mate ages. Their exact timings vary according to a personal chart.

# WOMAN'S MAGIC IN SPIRALS AND CYCLES

If you are keen to find out more about your own, then I recommend that you have your chart drawn up by a professional astrologer.

Whether you believe in astrology or not, it is interesting to notice the synchronistic role these planets play at major turning points in all our lives.

## The effects of the five outer planets

### JUPITER (12-year cycle):
ASSOCIATED WITH BENEVOLENCE, LEARNING, TRAVEL AND EXPANSION

*New cycles begin at approximate ages of 12, 24, 36, 48, 56, 72*

Jupiter takes twelve years to complete its travels around our natal chart. Consequently, every twelve years opportunities can arise for rapid expansion through work, travel or just plain good luck. It is worth remembering, however, that since it is the planet of expansion, Jupiter magnifies what is going on in our lives at that moment. This also means that we could fall into the danger of over-indulgence too. It is interesting to note, however, that many women feel very strong maternal instincts around the age of thirty-six if they have not had a child, while those approaching the age of forty-eight are often leaving behind the rigours of motherhood to expand their personal horizons in different directions.

### SATURN (28-year cycle):
ASSOCIATED WITH DISCIPLINE, KARMA AND PHYSICAL CRISIS

*New cycles begin at approximate ages of 28, 56, 84*

Saturn is known as the planet of personal karma. It makes us pay close attention to ourselves by setting up seemingly fated events through the relationships we draw into our lives. In short, Saturn is the great disciplinarian and teacher which gives us what we need in order for us to grow, rather than what we think we want at the time. Hence Saturn is often associated with physical and emotional loss, pain and depression if we are not willing to let go of worn-out beliefs or relationships which no longer serve us as we step into its new cycle.

- **Age of 28: 1st Saturn return** (effects last until approx. 32) The age of twenty-eight can be a highly volatile period which causes emotional challenges because Saturn makes us decide if we want to embrace responsibility and commitment, or need to end unsatisfactory relationships both at home and work. Consequently, many women who have married young find their first Saturn return particularly disturbing if their relationship is no longer fulfilling. By this time, they could well have children which means they have to come to terms with shouldering the responsibility of being a single parent. It also means that those women who have been alone in their twenties can suddenly find themselves in committed relationships.

- **Age of 56: 2nd Saturn return** (effects last until approx. 60) Traditionally this is the time for beginning to think about our retirement years and what we want to accomplish in them. We no longer want the challenges of our youth; instead we are subconsciously preparing for a time of reflection, and perhaps exploring the joys of becoming grandmothers.

  Our bodies are also changing shape because we are passing through the watershed of the menopause, and are facing new challenges to do with our self-image. This, therefore, is a time to explore our spiritual beliefs and allow ourselves to enter our mature years with dignity. When we remain in self-denial it brings about feelings of frustration, or a sense of desperately searching for something we can never find. Therefore this time can bring a great deal of personal anguish which needs to be faced and overcome. So, we can either become the hag of destruction, or embrace the wisdom of the crone.

● **Age of 84: 3rd Saturn return** This can bring a multitude of blessings to octogenarians, while also inciting intense anxiety in their offspring! Far from hanging up their boots, some women suddenly take on a new lease of life and can be found leaping out of aeroplanes, going on world cruises, and pursuing all manner of interests and hobbies – which can also include new spouses! I know of at least four women who have remarried in their late seventies or early eighties and are thoroughly enjoying it too. It is as if Saturn suddenly lifts the lid to allow us to enjoy a last shot at life. This final Saturn return also coincides with the return of Uranus to its natal position.

## URANUS (84-year cycle):
ASSOCIATED WITH SUDDEN CHANGE AND EMOTIONAL CRISIS
*Major effects take place during the square and opposition aspects at the ages of 21, 42, 63*

● **Age of 21: 1st Uranus square** Uranus makes its first square aspect around the age of twenty-one. Traditionally this is when we step away from our maidenhood to become young women. In this way, it pushes us out into life and away from the protection of our parents. It also provides us with a sense of rebellion

– of beginning to embark on the journey of
self-knowledge, albeit as an outward expression in the
world rather than as an inward experience. Think of the
hippies, punks and whatever fashionable trend springs to
mind. It is a time for young women to explore
themselves sexually and to assert themselves as people in
their own right within the confines and expectations of
society.

● **Age of 42: Uranus opposition with its natal
placement**   Our Uranus opposition brings with it the
infamous mid-life crisis. This is one of the most
challenging periods of our lives because the rebellious
energy of Uranus makes us reassess everything we have
and do. Many women will end their relationships
around this time because they desire a new way of
relating to the world at large. They may also find
themselves victims of marital breakdown which gives
them no choice but to make enormous changes in
their lives. If we are not aware of ourselves, and also of
our emotional needs, we may find ourselves searching
outside for the answers and becoming living
embodiments of Shirley Valentine.

Depression can also become a serious symptom at
this time, because we have to face the fact that we are
no longer able to compete with smooth-skinned young
beauties and often suffer the indignity of watching our
partners walking away with one on their arm. The
temptation to run to the nearest cosmetic surgeon and
to take HRT is ever present. However, when we can
come to terms with our ageing process, rather than
fighting it or denying it, we can begin to create a life
that is really fulfilling and indeed very blessed. In fact

many women only begin to achieve their true potential after they have been through this particular watershed.

- **Age of 63: 2nd Uranus square**   As Uranus brings an opportunity for re-orientation during our early forties, so it brings a spiritual crisis in our early sixties. If we have not taken on board the lessons of our mid-life crisis, this Uranus square can be experienced as a time of intense disillusionment and a feeling of having wasted our lives. Should this be the case, now is the time to start looking at spiritual beliefs and to put any wrongs to right within family relationships. In many indigenous cultures, this period of a woman's life is considered to be her wisdom years when she can provide valuable help and guidance to the younger women in her tribe. It is also a time when we can begin to gently consider how we want to prepare for the inevitability of our death.

- **Age of 84: Completion of Uranus cycle**   This is a time which accentuates our spiritual and emotional dimensions. It is therefore a fine opportunity to deal with any remaining unresolved issues and to make peace with ourselves and everyone around us. It is also time to give away treasured objects to those we love setting us free to concentrate on preparing ourselves for our death with wisdom, love and complete acceptance.

## NEPTUNE (146-year cycle):

ASSOCIATED WITH CONFUSION, DISSOLVING OR, AT ITS
HIGHER VIBRATION, UNCONDITIONAL LOVE

*Its opposition can be felt during our 70s and 80s*

Since Neptune's life cycle is so long, the influence of its opposition occurs later in life. At its highest vibration, it dissolves old ideas and visions of what life holds and enables us to see our past experiences from a much higher perspective. It also encourages us to turn inward to make peace with God. In this way it dissolves the veil between the seen and unseen worlds so we can prepare ourselves for the great transition and open our hearts to receive the unconditional love of the universe. However, if we are consumed with fear and resistance to the unknown, it marks a time when mental delusion and confusion sets in.

## PLUTO (248-year cycle):

ASSOCIATED WITH DEATH AND REBIRTH

Pluto is a slow mover; its task is to break down all our outmoded beliefs so the phoenix can rise from the ashes. It shakes us up, and makes us take responsibility for who we really are. This can happen at any time of life. Pluto's effects can especially be felt as it forms an aspect (square, opposition or conjunction) with a natal planet, or the ascendant (personal transformation), descendant (transformation of relationships), mid-heaven (transformation in career) or nadir (transformation in home environment). Its powerful energy often manifests as challenging external influences (accidents, death of loved ones and so on) or relationships with people who will have a radical effect on us. These folk may well disappear as quickly as they arrived, leaving what seems like a trail of devastation in our lives. Their job, however, is done; they have shaken us to the core of our being and life will never be the same again. It is up to us to interpret the lesson they provided and to change our lifestyles accordingly.

## Table of planetary influences

| Approx. age | Planet position | Influence |
|---|---|---|
| 12 | 1st Jupiter return | Onset of puberty |
| 21 | 1st Uranus square | Identity crisis/ rebellion/assertion |
| 24 | 2nd Jupiter return | Opportunity to expand identity |
| 28/32 | 1st Saturn return | Challenge/responsibility/ new phase |
| 36 | 3rd Jupiter return | Opportunity for new self-expression |
| 42 | Uranus opposition | Mid-life crisis/personal re-evaluation |
| 48 | 4th Jupiter return | Opportunity for new self-expression |
| 56/60 | 2nd Saturn return | Breakdown of old ideals/new phase |
| 60 | 5th Jupiter return | Opportunity for new self-expression |
| 63+ | 2nd Uranus square | Spiritual evaluation |
| 72 | 6th Jupiter return | Opportunity to expand inner life |
| Late 70s+ | Neptune opposition | Shift in consciousness |
| 84+ | 1st Uranus return | Acceleration of spirituality |
| 85 | 3rd Saturn return | New lease of life! |

## The cycles of the moon

The moon's passage around our charts also affects us at key points in our lives. This follows the same time frame as the twenty-eight-year cycle of Saturn, adding to the intensity of those experiences

in seven-year periods. Every seven years, the moon squares or
opposes its natal placement which brings us some kind of emotional crisis or challenge. This is where the infamous 'seven-year
itch' comes from. As the moon completes each cycle it too presents us with a new opportunity for emotional maturity.

## Table of lunar influence

| Approx. age | Moon position | Influence |
| --- | --- | --- |
| 7 | Moon square | Emotionally beginning to break from mother |
| 14 | Moon opposition | Emotions intensified through puberty |
| 21 | Moon square | Emotional crisis – entering adulthood |
| **28** | **1st Moon return** | **Emotional responsibility for self and others** |
| 35 | Moon square | Emotional crisis if needs are not being met |
| 42 | Moon opposition | Emotional crisis if not fulfilled creatively |
| 49 | Moon square | Emotionally paying for unresolved issues |
| **56** | **2nd Moon return** | **Emotions peak, new cycle begins** |
| 63 | Moon square | Emotionally coming to terms with life path |
| 70 | Moon opposition | Emotionally reflective |
| 77 | Moon square | Emotional shift towards greater consciousness |
| **84** | **3rd Moon return** | **Higher emotional perspective** |

# Numerology: the Intelligence of the Heart

Now for some practical fun! It is really easy to work out your numbers even if, like me, you have always been hopeless at maths. First, here's a potted history of numerology so you not only understand what you are working with, but also realise the power of its origins.

The universe vibrates with sound, and from sound all things manifest in one form or another. Vibrational sound can smash solid items to smithereens or lull a person into peaceful slumbers. Yet the true language of vibration is mathematics – the science of numbers. Mathematics gives order to the universe and provides vibration with a structure from which geometry (Latin for measurement) is derived. Geometry is the foundation for all human-made structures. However, the great mystics and esoteric teachers of the ancient world, including the Chaldeans, Phoenicians, Babylonians, Hindus, Chinese, Mayans and American Indians, also knew how to use mathematics to access the hidden depths of the metaphysical world. The priests of Memphis, the ancient capital of Egypt, are recorded as saying that 'the ancient science of numbers and the art of will power are the keys of magic that open the gates of the universe'. The Greeks called the study of numbers 'pure reason'; the Egyptians called it 'the intelligence of the heart'; and in India, it is still referred to as 'heart–mind'. This is because the study of esoteric numerology involved both sides of the brain: the left to receive the logical facts and the right side to attune to the occult significance.

## The influence of Pythagorus

Pythagorus, the father of modern mathematics (c.600 BC), considered that numbers were the principle of everything. He had a revelation from observing the circular movement of the heavens that each world had its own way of being, yet everything moved together in total harmony. The universe was, in fact, a proportion, or number, in itself; in which case the essence of numbers was the very foundation of everything. This led him to realise that humankind lived in three essential dimensions: the natural world; the material world; the divine world. Although humankind could embrace many forms of teachings and beliefs, there was, in reality, only one divine spirit. This divinity could be found in every facet of existence. In this way, Pythagorus taught his pupils the importance of embracing and accepting the physical reality while working towards the divine.

Pythagorus discovered that one to nine were the primary numbers of the universal law, which when attributed to humankind, represents inner spiritual qualities. Here is a very basic outline of what each number resonates to:

1 Leadership, individuality, courage and determination
2 Patience, family, harmony, co-operation, partnerships, money
3 Expression, joy, creativity, love affairs, expansion, pregnancy
4 Foundation, discipline, construction, hard work
5 Change, travel, freedom, spontaneity, communication
6 Nurturing, service, work, love, family, teaching, healing
7 Studiousness, knowledge, spirituality, aloneness, seeking
8 Practicality, authority, business practice, ambition, abundance
9 Benevolence, completion, drama, artistry, colour, friendships

Each person is born into one of the nine vibrations and this is their personal life path number. This is very simple to work out. Here is an example:

You need to write down your date of birth in numbers, placing the month **before** the day:

For example: February 3, 1953

February is the second month and therefore = **2**
The day of birth is the third and therefore = **3**
The year is 1953. Add these numbers together like this: 1+9+5+3= 18.
Now add 18 together: 1+8 = **9**

Now add your three primary numbers together:
**2 + 3 + 9** = 14
Add 14 together: 1 + 4 = **5**
**The number 5 is the personal birth path number**

This person is therefore governed by the expression of 5 which is to do with change, travel, freedom, communication and spontaneity – which is a very accurate assessment considering she is not only a writer, traveller and teacher, but also a contrary, freedom-loving Aquarian!

The mystical meaning of all nine numbers can be incorporated into anything you want to make sacred or special. This can include house numbers, telephone numbers, the number of your own name, numbers to use in ritual, or to grasp a deeper understanding of your own personal destiny. In parallel with astrology, numerology is one of the great occult sciences, so if you are drawn to it, there any plenty of good books available on the subject.

## THE MYSTICAL SIGNIFICANCE
## OF THE NINE-YEAR CYCLE

Pythagorus also believed that everything in the universe was influenced by progressive circles or spirals, which he measured by using the nine numbers. Following this theory he attributed these nine numbers to the life cycles of humanity. This became the foundation for his science of numerology – and the key for interpreting our destiny.

Again this is simple to work out as in the example below.

---

For example: February 3, 1953

February is the second month and therefore = **2**
The day of birth is the third and therefore = **3**
The year is 1953. Add these numbers together like this:
1+9+5+3= 18. Now add 18 together: 1 + 8 = **9**

Now add your three primary numbers together:
**2** + **3**+ **9** = 14
Add 14 together: 1 + 4 = **5**

Your personal birth path number also indicated what year of your nine-year cycle you were born into.

Therefore this person was born into the **fifth year** of their first nine-year cycle.

Age in years        0 1 2 3 4 5 6 7 8 9 10 11 12 13 14 15 etc.
Birth path cycle    5 6 7 8 9 1 2 3 4 5 6 7 8 9 1 2 etc.

This person started their second nine-year cycle at the age of five.

---

# WOMAN'S MAGIC IN SPIRALS AND CYCLES

## HOW TO WORK OUT WHICH CYCLE YOU ARE IN

It is just as easy to work out which year of your personal nine-year cycle you are currently experiencing. All you have to do is add the month and day of your birthday to the current year. (Each nine-year cycle begins on 1 January.) Here is an example:

---

Add month and day of birth together: February 3, 1953
February = 2
Day of birth = 3
2 + 3 = 5

Now add together the numbers of the current year:
For example: 1999
1+9+9+9= 28
Add 28 together: 2 + 8 = 10. Now add 10 together:
1 + 0 = 1

Now add the 5 from the month and day of your birth to current year number: 5 + 1 = 6

This person is now experiencing the influence of the **sixth year** of their personal cycle.

---

## THE MYSTICAL INFLUENCE OF THE NINE-YEAR CYCLES

Each individual year draws to it a different experience:

**1st year** (governed by the sun): New beginnings, making plans, letting go of the past. Strength of purpose and organisational abilities are needed because this can be a testing time when starting out afresh.
**2nd year** (governed by the moon): This can often be a time of gestation or waiting for something to come to the

boil, therefore it brings lessons of patience. It can also bring romantic partnerships, new friends and instil harmony into relationships.

**3rd year** (governed by Jupiter): This is a year of expansion and for creative ideas and knowledge to flourish. Travel is also indicated alongside the possibility of passionate love affairs and pregnancy!

**4th year** (governed by Uranus): This creates a grounding for all those ideas, which means it is a year of practical hard work, resolve and responsibility. It is also a time to make sure the foundations of your life are well and truly in place before you enter into the second half of this present cycle which pushes everything up a notch.

**5th year** (governed by Mercury): This is the year of change and the watershed of the cycle. It tests our relationships both at home and at work, while presenting us with the opportunity to transform ourselves and free up our spirits. It can bring about house moves, extended travel and new work and relationship opportunities.

**6th year** (governed by Venus): Six is the number of love and domesticity. Therefore, issues to do with service to family as well as society will surface. It also intensifies the work ethic, but alongside this travels love and romance. It is a wonderful year to embark on a new relationship or recommit to an existing one.

**7th year** (governed by Neptune): This is a year for reflection and introspection. It is a time to assess our spiritual beliefs and to ascertain what is important to us. It draws study of a higher nature, and therefore a deep-hearted wish for peace and tranquillity.

**8th year** (governed by Saturn): Saturn is the task master, and 8 the number of abundance and growth. Therefore this year is about ambition and solidifying financial assets. It is also the year for business acquisitions, mergers and expansion to take place, and is especially beneficial for setting up any new venture.

**9th year** (governed by Mars): The number 9 marks completion as this particular cycle draws to a close. It can therefore be a time of clearing out anything which no longer is of benefit to us, which can include relationships as well as working environments. Therefore, this is not a particularly auspicious time for starting new enterprises or indeed relationships. These new ventures ideally need to wait for the arrival of the new first-year cycle.

Each nine-year cycle we enter gives us the opportunity to reassess how we want to live our lives and to make those necessary adjustments in order for us to reach our highest potential as human beings. By becoming aware of what year we are entering, we can also make full use of its influences.

As we gain wisdom through our life's experiences we can shed our burdens of guilt, shame and despair and this in turn allows us the room for the healing process to begin. This is how enlightenment occurs, and it is as if our nine-year cycles are indeed spirals which propel us ever onwards towards the unconditional love of the Divine.

# Chapter 6
# Woman's Magic and the Goddess

**T**HE DIVINE DUALITY OF the masculine and feminine in the form of gods and goddesses has played a major part in the spiritual evolution of humankind since the dawn of time. In Eastern religions, their gods and goddesses continue to be the subject of worship and adornment. This was our way too in the old times, and thankfully it is still kept alive through pagan traditions.

The concept that the physical world was, in fact, divine duality incarnate on earth was deemed to be so fearsome and awesome that humanity created the perfect solution to explain it: archetypes. These archetypes were transposed into heavenly beings, the mythological gods and goddesses themselves who were to become central characters in the great tales and heroic sagas. These sagas represented the many different facets of human behaviour; of good overcoming evil and of love conquering hate. They also represented the different essences of the natural world which could either help or hinder the quest of humankind. In this guise they became real external forces which required veneration and appeasement in order for life to survive. So, particularly during the Greek and Roman dynasties, great temples were constructed and dedicated in their honour. The myths which built up around these deities are quite wonderful, and well worth looking into as part of the journey towards understanding the role of Goddess, and yourself as an expression of the divine feminine.

# The Six Major Goddesses

In classical mythology, there were six main goddesses alive in our psyches.

## Femininity and the wife

**Hera** (Greek)                                    **Juno** (Roman)

Hera was the greatest and one of the most terrible of the Olympian goddesses. She was also wife to Zeus, God of Gods. She became embittered by Zeus's many infidelities and summarily persecuted his mistresses and offspring. She was also responsible for rendering Tiresias blind when he sided with Zeus in the argument that women derived far more pleasure from sex than men! The Roman goddess Juno was depicted as much softer, and therefore the symbol of femininity and married virtue.

Hera's usual symbol is the peacock, the plumage of which is said to represent the eyes of Argos, her faithful servant. Hera granted Argos immortality by moving his eyes to the tail feathers of the peacock after he had been killed by Hermes. Hermes had been dispatched by Zeus to rescue Io, yet another of his lovers, from the hundred watchful eyes of Argos. The peacock feather is often considered to be a symbol of vainglory, while in some Eastern traditions it is a mark of rank. The peacock tail gained its reputation of being the 'evil eye' because of its association with Hera's jealousy and Argus as the ever-vigilant traitor according to Zeus.

### EVOKING HERA OR JUNO
Since Hera is such a powerful and vengeful goddess she needs to be treated with a modicum of respect! I would suggest calling on

her powers when you need courage to overcome some seemingly insurmountable obstacle, or when you are facing a particularly physical challenge such as mountain-climbing, or marathon-running. Her strength and determination will be perfect allies.

Juno, however, is quite different because she is much sweeter and kinder. Since she is the symbol of fidelity and virtue, she is perfect to evoke when entering into a new partnership or to bless your marriage vows. According to legend, Juno also watched over childbirth. It was forbidden for any woman to wear a knotted belt who came to place an offering at her altar on behalf of a woman in labour, since this could cause problems for her during delivery. Juno was the protector of all facets of a woman's life, particularly when married. In pagan traditions, knot magic is often used to aid childbirth. The knots are symbolically untied, and windows and doors are thrown open at the start of labour pains.

In Roman mythology all men were accompanied by their personal *genius* or spirit guardian from cradle to grave. This *genius* governed their fate and fortune, as well as forming their character and personality. For a woman, this was replaced by her own personal *juno* or divine double which personified and protected her femininity.

## Mother Earth

**Demeter** (Greek)                    **Ceres** (Roman)

Demeter was the mother of Persephone whom she lost to Hades, Lord of the Underworld, for six months of the year. During this time of waiting for her beloved daughter to return to life, she commanded that all should die on the earth's surface and thus the six months of winter were created. The Roman goddess Ceres was her equivalent, and also known as the Goddess of the Corn which has given us the word *cereal*. Demeter's name is derived from the Indo-European word *meter* which gives many languages their word for mother. Demeter is usually symbolised as sitting holding torches or a serpent, whereas Ceres is portrayed with sheaves of corn. Demeter's personality is distinctly different from that of Gaia, the Great Provider, who we met in Chapter 1. Gaia is considered to be the personification of the holistic cosmology of the earth itself, while Demeter is the representation of agriculture and fertility of the land.

## EVOKING DEMETER

Demeter is perfect to call upon to take care of your garden during planting time, and to be general overseer of your flowers, plants and vegetables. It is therefore a delightful idea to create some sort of shrine to her in a shady nook or beneath a tree. You can place offerings of fruit and vegetables as a gesture of thanks throughout the year, and pay special attention to her on the four great pastoral sabbats which mark the changing of the seasons:

### SAMHAIN (31 October) Symbol: apple

This is the official pagan New Year and traditionally known as All Hallow's Eve. *Samhain* is an old Celtic word which means *summer's end*. Since it marked the death of the year, it was also known as the Festival of the Dead, the night when the veil between the seen and unseen worlds is at its thinnest. Great bonfires were lit to pave the way for those who had died during the year as they travelled into the world of spirit. Apples were piled on to altars to provide sustenance for these souls and so, in addition, Samhain was known as the Festival of Apples.

### IMBOLC (2 February) Symbol: snowdrops and honey

This traditionally symbolises the beginning of spring and the start of the ewes' lactation. In fact, the word *Imbolc* is derived from *oimelc* meaning *ewe's milk*. This time is also known as Candlemas or the Festival of Lights which celebrates the appearance of snowdrops. Candles were lit to show that Persephone was once again returning to the surface of the earth, with her mother celebrating this by allowing the sun to warm the land again in preparation for new growth and fertility. Traditionally this was the day when priestesses were initiated into their traditions and offered honey to symbolise the sweetness of the Goddess.

## BELTAINE (30 April) Symbol: hawthorn blossom

Beltaine comes from the name of the Celtic sky god Bel and the Welsh word *tan* meaning *fire*. It is the start of summer, and the eve when young people would come together to jump the fires to symbolise hand-fasting rituals. It was also the night when the Stag King and May Queen came together sexually to represent the divine duality of the gods and goddesses who placed blessings of fertility on the land and people. Hawthorn blossom was used prolifically to decorate homes and maypoles to symbolise fertility, happiness and protection against the evil eye. It is dedicated to Hymen, God of Marriage, Flora, Goddess of Flowers and Carna, a wood nymph who protected virginity. It is said that when a suitor pursued her, she would lead him into her sacred woods and then disappear. Until, that is, Janus, God of All Doorways, Gates and Entrances, fell in love with her. He finally overcame her behind a rock where she was hiding. To pacify her and make amends, Janus (January is named after him) gave her blossom from the hawthorn which was imbued with magical powers to ward off evil from any doorways or openings of houses. As such, Carna was especially evoked to ward off vampires.

## LAMMAS (1 August) Symbol: corn wreath, bread

Lughnasagh, as Lammas is also known, is the celebration of Lugh, the Celtic sun god, who dies as the year begins to turn towards winter, and the corn is harvested in the fields. Lammas comes from the Saxon *hlaf-mass* which means *festival of bread*. Great feasts were held in honour of Ceres and Demeter to give thanks for an abundant harvest and to bless the seeds for the following year. Corn wreaths also were made and paraded in the streets by farm workers to symbolise the death of the corn god and the grief of Demeter as Persephone prepared to return to the underworld.

## The moon

### Artemis (Greek)                    Diana (Roman)

Artemis was always depicted as an untameable virgin girl, fiercely protective of her chastity, the personification of hunting – mortals and stags – and said to inflict pain on women who died in childbirth. Regarded as the twin sister of the sun god Apollo, she was automatically connected with the power of the moon. She was also considered by some to represent the maiden aspect of the triple vision of the Goddess, although many prefer Persephone as the maiden aspect, due to her association with love. So Artemis was closely connected with Hecate, the crone aspect of the Goddess and patron Goddess of Magic and Witchcraft. Artemis never married, and spurned domestic life as well as love affairs. She dwelt in the mountains of Arcadia accompanied by her hounds and her hand maidens, and was renowned as a ferocious warrioress. As such, she was adopted by the Amazons as their protector because they too were huntresses and warrioresses independent of men. The equivalent in Roman culture was Diana whose sacred animal was a hind, or small female red deer. She too brought death to women through natural causes, and became the champion of those warrioresses and huntresses who maintained autonomy from men.

### EVOKING ARTEMIS

Artemis is a powerful goddess to evoke for those of you who choose to live independently of men, or have decided against marriage. She is, therefore, a very strong force in the gay pagan movement. You can also call on her energy when you are facing sexual discrimination in the workplace, or you find yourself being persecuted for any reason. Her power would be enough to set most people quaking in their shoes! I would call on the energy of Artemis if I found I was facing a life-threatening situation through physical attack or if I needed an extra burst of energy to get me out of danger. She would also be useful if you need to single-mindedly focus your attention on achieving a goal or career – or when you need to stand your ground against other people's opinions. She will provide the strength for you to stand up for yourself.

Artemis is a goddess not to be taken lightly and I would recommend that should you work with her energy, please be respectful of it.

## Wisdom

**Athena** (Greek)                              **Minerva** (Roman)

Athena is the warrioress goddess who sprang from the head of Zeus, armed with her spear and 'aegis' – a shield shrouded by fear, strife, force and pursuit, in the centre of which was a gorgon's head given to her by Perseus. She is the personification of wisdom and of placing principle above passion, as well as being Goddess of Arts and Crafts including those of war. She became patron Goddess of Athens and protector of warriors, representing political intrigue rather than violence. It was reputed that she possessed grey eyes, and was accompanied by her power totem, the owl, which has always been associated with wisdom. Minerva was her Roman counterpart, also portrayed in military garb of helmet and armour.

# WOMAN'S MAGIC AND THE GODDESS

### EVOKING ATHENA

Athena is usually shown bearing a spear or sword – which is seen to be the symbol of truth and justice. She therefore personifies clear thinking and rational thought which are valuable assets when any kind of trouble brews in relation to legal issues. Sometimes it is very difficult to find the way out of emotionally-charged situations, therefore her energy is particularly beneficial to clear the way. I would suggest calling on her help if, for example, you are splitting up a relationship which looks as if it could turn into a traumatic court battle, or when you are facing emotionally-based problems in a working situation. I would also call on her when you need to find an inner strength and resolve to commit to something which is going to push you to your limits. Perhaps this is a new business venture where considerable risk is needed in order to get it off the ground, or you have decided to start your life afresh in a different country. Since Athena is associated with the owl – a bird of night which can see and hunt in the dark – she may well appear in your dreams to provide guidance and answers. So, keep a pen and paper beside your bed.

## Love

**Aphrodite** (Greek)                      **Venus** (Roman)

Aphrodite is the most famous goddess of all since she is the one to grant love or take it away. She is also the goddess of free love, said to have risen from the foam produced by the genitals of Uranus which had fallen into the sea after being severed by his son, Cronus. The name Aphrodite is possibly connected to *aphros*, the Greek word for foam. Aphrodite was married to Hephaestus or Vulcan in Roman mythology. Although ugly, he was an extremely skilled smithy and gentle by nature. However, Aphrodite's beauty was to cause havoc for all those who beheld her. Indeed her beauty was to be the prime cause of the Trojan Wars. The three great goddesses, Hera, Athena and Aphrodite, called on the services of Paris to judge who was the most fair. Poor Paris, understandably, was not keen to take on this role but eventually he succumbed. Hera told him that he could rule the world if he chose her; Athena promised to make him the mightiest warrior; but Aphrodite simply opened her gown, promised him love and the hand in marriage of the most beautiful woman in the world if he chose her. There was no competition after that! The prize for Paris was to be Helen of Troy who, unfortunately, was already married to Menelaus – and he had no intention of giving her up. So the Trojan Wars began. Aphrodite had many affairs, but her greatest love was Ares, God of War. Their names were changed to Mars and Venus during the Roman dynasty, and Venus's name was immortalised through the appearance of the morning or evening star depending on the time of year. The original symbol of Mars was the cross of matter above the circle of spirit, while the symbol of Venus is the circle of spirit standing on the cross of matter. Placed together 'foot to foot', they are the perfect representation of 'as above, so below'. Fathered by Mercury, Venus also gave birth to Cupid. Her chief festival was on 1 April and her element became copper because mirrors were traditionally made from it.

## EVOKING APHRODITE OR VENUS

When we fall in love, we have much to learn about ourselves. This is because love is full of illusion. The person we unconsciously draw to us mirrors back exactly who we are at that given moment, warts and all, so we need to rise above equating initial sexual passion with love. This kind of love disappears in a puff of wind. Aphrodite can indeed be called upon to bring love into your life – but you must be prepared to face the consequences. Love never appears without considerable personal challenges and lessons to be learnt. Nevertheless, when you have a deep union with your partner, nothing is more rewarding, and the potential for spiritual growth is enormous. In the words of Meher Baba: 'A relationship that deals with truth walks the fine line between chaos and cosmos all the time.' If you are having problems in your relationship, or you need to make important decisions which will affect your relationship, evoke the power of Aphrodite to guide you through the mire. I would also recommend creating a small shrine to her somewhere in your home. It doesn't have to be very complicated but it will remind you that love needs to be nurtured and cared for if it is to blossom. You can also call on the energy of Aphrodite to help in any decision-making, especially if you are susceptible to the illusion of glamour.

## Domestic life and purity

**Hestia** (Greek)                    **Vesta (as in vestal)** (Roman)

Hestia was granted special favours by Zeus who allowed her to keep her virginity and tend the hearth of Olympus itself. Thus the hearth became the religious focus in temples and homes. According to Roman legend, Vesta was the custodian of the sacred fire brought from Troy which was never allowed to go out since this would bring disaster. The Romans created the cult of the goddess Vesta in which vestal virgin priestesses tended her perpetual to make sure the fires in the city blazed as brightly. These vestal virgins were daughters of nobility who began their training as young as six. They underwent rigorous discipline and remained in service for up to thirty years. Great talisman significance was attached to the perpetual flame throughout the Roman dynasty, and fire rituals were used throughout the empire as part of goddess worship.

### EVOKING HESTIA

It is a wonderful gesture to evoke the blessings of Hestia into your home to grant it protection, harmony and peace. It is also respectful to remember her when you light a fire in the hearth. You can also symbolically light a candle to her if you have no hearth. Her energy reminds us that we need to be constantly vigilant about our own inner home fires: without warmth in our soul, we become like the living dead. You can also evoke Hestia if you want to find a new home. Give her your 'shopping list' and then leave it up to her. The right place will manifest at exactly the right moment and in the most magical way. If you have a mantlepiece over a fireplace, you can transform it into a shrine for her which will remind you every day of what you need to do for yourself in order to keep your own fire alight.

It is said that all these mighty goddesses, their spouses and lovers dined on ambrosia, supped nectar and their ethereal blood was made of colourless 'ichor'. And long may they preside over us!

## The Minor Goddesses

The minor goddesses played an equally important role in classical mythology, and here are just a few of them who still influence our language today:

| | |
|---|---|
| Human soul | **Psyche**, the Greek personification of the human soul with whom Eros fell in love. |
| Divine retribution | **Nemesis**, the Greek goddess who curbs excess such as false pride and extreme good fortune. |
| Marriage | **Hymen** (or **Hymenaeus**) is in fact a god. It is said that he led wedding processions, and was so beautiful that he was generally |

mistaken for a girl. Through a heroic deed to gain the hand of the maiden he loved, his memory was always invoked during wedding ceremonies as a gesture of good luck. Some legends say he tragically died on his own wedding day which is why his name has become synonymous with marriage. His attributes were a torch and a crown of flowers, which is why it is traditional for brides to wear flowers in their hair.

Health    **Hygenia** was the daughter of Asclepius, God of Medicine, who was the son of Apollo.

Breeze    **Aura**, Goddess of the Wind, who fell into madness.

Dawn    **Aurora**, the mother of the four winds, who opened the gates of heaven to the chariot of the sun with 'rosy' fingers.

Rainbows    **Iris**, usually portrayed with wings and dressed in silk, was the messenger of the gods, particularly associated with Hera and Zeus.

Spring    **Flora**, Goddess of Plants and Flowers, who possesses the power to make the blossom grow. April is her sacred month and honey is her gift to humankind.

Harmony    **Harmonia**, the love child of Aphrodite, Goddess of Love, and Ares, God of War.

Gardens    **Pomona**, Roman nymph of fruit, who lived in a sacred wood called Pomonal on the road from Rome. She was linked with fertility and the cycles of nature.

Echo    **Echo**, the nymph who, on being spurned by

|   | Narcissus, faded away until only a shadow of her voice was left. |
|---|---|
| Easter | **Oestre**, Goddess of the Spring Equinox, who renews life, and whose sacred power animal is the hare. |
| The earth | **Gaia**, the Greek goddess of the earth, whom we met in Chapter 1. |
| Hexing | **Hecate**, the Greek queen of witchcraft and the underworld who wreaked havoc for travellers at crossroads with her company of baying dogs. |
| Misfortune | **Pandora**, the Greek name of the first woman to bring misfortune to humankind as her box carried such ills as work and disease. |
| Siren | **The Sirens** were a group of women in Greek myth who lured passing seamen to their destruction with their beautiful songs. |
| Spider's webs | **Arachne** wove such beautiful embroidery that the nymphs came to gaze upon her work. A violently jealous Athena, also Goddess of Spinners and Embroiders, finally stabbed her with a shuttle. Arachne hanged herself in despair, but Athena changed her into a spider which continues to weave the web of life for eternity. |

You may feel a special resonance with some of these goddesses, or you may feel more affinity with those from different parts of the world. It doesn't matter. The important thing is to be open to these energies in whatever guise they appear to you. The concept of the Goddess is alive in all women irrespective of culture or religious persuasion. Accepting her as part of ourselves is an important part of our spiritual initiation and evolution. It may well be that you become particularly attached to a certain goddess, or one will appear to you during a meditation at different times of your life. For example, Athena made herself known to me when I was going through an important life change. Since that took place, I have not felt a need to work with her energy although I know she is still within my psyche which provides me with a strong sense of self.

## Finding Your Sacred Name

Finding your sacred name is very much part of your initiation process, another way of getting in touch with who you are. Secret power names have been used for thousands of years. The occult name would be granted by the tribal elders at a young child's naming ceremony after they had witnessed its special characteristics or habit through a vision or dream. The name would remain secret until the child reached puberty whereupon it would be spoken for the first time in public to acknowledge that the child was ready to step into the responsibility of adulthood.

Some people receive their sacred name by following spiritual masters. I have been at Celtic naming ceremonies where people have received theirs through the vision of the officiating priest and priestess. In my own case, I discovered my sacred name many years ago through a very deep meditation when I first started out on my spiritual quest. As soon as I heard the name, my heart leapt for joy. It felt so completely appropriate. I always feel deeply empowered by thinking of it and, when the chips are down, it provides me with extra will and courage to carry on. I have chosen not to share my name with many people. It is just too personal, and I respect it too much for it to be uttered on a whim. You may feel differently about this, as do many of my friends who have legally changed to their sacred name.

Here is a ritual meditation which you can use to receive your sacred name.

## Sacred naming ritual

Since this is such a personal and powerful journey into the light of your soul, it is worth preparing yourself for it properly. Make sure you clean your home thoroughly by smudging it with sage smoke, and ask for the blessings of the Goddess to be granted. Next bathe yourself as if you were preparing for your own baptism, and dress in clothing which makes you feel beautiful. Prepare an altar with two silver candles and a vase of your favourite fresh flowers. Burn frankincense on a charcoal block which will heighten your senses and aid your meditation process.

When you feel ready, light your candles in honour of the Goddess, and ask that your sacred name be revealed to you. Close your eyes, and take a few moments to relax into yourself. When you feel ready, ask for your guide to appear in your mind's eye, and take you into your life spiral. As you look forward, you see a light beckoning to you. This is the light of your true potential of being a woman in this lifetime. As your guide escorts you towards this light, you begin to feel the reverence of what you are doing. By taking a sacred name, you will walk in the footsteps of the Goddess.

As you reach the light you can feel it enfolding you and loving you. Allow yourself to surrender into it and then open your heart to receive it. Feel it washing your doubts away and allow it to cleanse the whole of your body. It becomes like an enormous, gushing waterfall, pouring over your head. Stretch up your arms and feel the sensation of the water – the power and magnificence of it. Before you is a beautiful pool set in a forest clearing.

Exotic birds and animals come down to the edge of the pool to savour its waters, and wonderful insects hover over the surface. There are also water lilies and an abundance of incredible flowers growing in and around the pool. It is a place of utter beauty, peace and serenity, and you know instinctively that this is the holy place where you will receive the baptism of your sacred name. As you walk into the pool, its warm, crystal clear waters receive you, and draw you under the surface. You are now in the realm of the undines. They take your hands and lead you deeper and deeper into the waters. You see ahead a magnificent throne, upon which sits a resplendent high priestess dressed in shimmering white robes. In her right hand she holds her staff of office, and to her left sits her sacred power animal. You are invited to kneel before her and, as you do so, by way of welcome and recognition she taps her staff lightly upon your right shoulder and then upon your left. She knows why you have come to her. She asks you to look into her eyes and, as you do so, she leans forward and, with her left hand, she places your sacred name into your heart. You feel your sacred name sinking into your heart, and beginning to glow and radiate a tremendous sense of power, integrity and personal pride. She now invites you to look into your heart to receive your name. This may come as a vision, as a feeling, or you may actually hear it. If nothing comes, you understand that it is not the moment for you to receive your sacred name, but it is there waiting in your heart to be revealed to you when the time is right.

Allow yourself to savour your sacred name, to feel it enveloping you like a protective mantle. This is your true vibration which has guided you throughout your life. Feel the magnificence of it, and honour yourself for being

ready to receive it. You also understand that from this
moment on you are willing to take complete responsibility
for yourself and everything that happens in your life, and
to work in service of the Goddess for the benefit of
humankind. The high priestess places her forefinger lightly
on your third eye and you feel her power radiating into
your body. You are now one with the divine force of all
things. You receive a vision of your mission upon the
earth; of how you can use your vibration as a daughter of
light to spread knowledge and love to those in fear. The
high priestess embraces you in welcome and, as she does
so, her power animal escorts your own sacred power
animal to your side. This is to be your guiding spirit for
the rest of your earthly life, and one that will protect and
defend you at all times. You and your power animal pay
homage to the high priestess, and allow the undines to
take you back to the surface of the pool. As you break
through the surface, you feel a surge of inner strength and
resolve such as you have never felt before. You feel
yourself shimmering in the light of the high priestess, and
feel cleansed of your negative patterns which have held
you back from being a truly magnificent woman. You
experience a sense of deep peace and serenity, and a
complete acceptance that your life will continue to evolve
into one of service to the Divine. Your power animal is
happy to remain at your sacred pool and, whenever you
need its guidance, you understand that you can return here
to find it.

When you are ready, walk through the waterfall, and
slowly begin to feel yourself back in your body and living
in the present. Open your eyes, and if you feel it is
appropriate, write about your journey. Allow the two
silver candles on your altar to burn down in their entirety,

so make sure they are in a safe place and away from draughts.

This is a very powerful ritual, which fundamentally changes something inside your psyche. Therefore, you may find in a short space of time, you begin to see the world around you with different eyes. This could influence your relationships as well as your working situation. If doors begin to close, or relationships break up, you will need to trust that everything is happening for your highest good, and that new avenues, which perhaps you have never considered before, will be opening up. Working with the Divine means letting go of the reins and trusting that you will be taken to the place you are meant to be. It also means opening up to the bigger vision; there could be a very good reason for you to experience certain relationships or circumstances before you find the right partner or avenue of work. Embracing your sacred name, and forging a link with your totem animal, will imbue you with a sense of personal pride which will help you overcome many an obstacle.

# Chapter 7
# Woman's Magic and the Sisterhood

**T**HE SISTERHOOD! WHERE WOULD we be without each other? I for one would have gone mad without the support, love and understanding of my girlfriends. Women are natural communicators, this is our inherent gift, and one that needs to be used to cement enduring friendships and relationships.

## The Origins of Sisterhood

The origins of sisterhood began when the men went hunting, leaving the women behind to tend to home matters as well as the crops in order for the tribe to survive. However, it was particularly during times of war when their men would be away for years at a time that the women banded together to become a force for their enemies to reckon with. During the Crusades up to 500,000 men were fighting in the Holy Lands, leaving the safe keeping of their land and titles in the hands of their wives.

One such noble lady was Lady Alice Knyvet of England who uttered these words in the face of her foe:

I will not leave possession of this castle to die therefore;
and if you begin to break the peace or make war to get the
place of me, I shall defend me. For rather I in such wise to

die than to be slain when my husband cometh home, for
he charged me to keep it.

It was also during this period that Blanche of Castile (1187–1251),
Queen of Louis VIII of France, became regent while her son,
King Louis IX, went to fight in the Holy Lands. It was because of
Blanche's abilities to suppress rebellions, and actually extend the
French dynasty by making powerful alliances with her neighbours,
that France is the country it is today.

Yet another great lady who stood her ground against all
adversity was Lady Mary Bankes of Corfe Castle in Dorset. During
the year of 1643, she steadfastly defended the castle against
tumultuous assaults from the Roundheads while her husband, Sir
John Bankes, was away. On his death in 1644, she again held out:

> . . . The other assaults the upper ward, which the Lady
> Bankes (to her eternal honour be it spoken) with her
> daughters, women and five soldiers, undertook to make
> good against the rebels, and did bravely perform what she
> undertook; for by heaving over stones and hot embers they
> repelled the rebels and kept them from climbing the
> ladders, thence to throw in that wildfire which every rebel
> had already in his hand.

Heroines come in all shapes and sizes, and among my own
personal favourites is that wonderful rapacious queen of early
Britain, Boudicca. What a sight she must have been, adorned with
horned helmet, driving her chariot straight at her enemy with
knives lashed to the wheels. However, the person I most resonate
with is Hildegard of Bingen who obviously possessed the energy
and tenacity of the goddess Athena in her soul. Born in 1098,
Hildegard became a German Benedictine nun as a young woman.
She spent the first half of her life in quiet devotion, and by her late

thirties had become the prioress of her convent. However, during her forty-third year, she began to experience prophetic visions and dreams which completely turned her life upside down. (This is a perfect example of a Uranus opposition creating a mid-life crisis.) Virtually overnight she became a strident warrioress fighting corruption in the established church and completely reforming monastic life. She also began to voraciously study scientific and medical topics (very Uranian), as well as composing sacred cantors which are still sung today. Hildegard finally founded her own impressive convent in 1147 at Rupertsberg which she personally helped to design and build. She finally died in her eighties, having established herself as one of the most prolific fighters for social reform the world has ever known. In one of her poems she describes a mystical vision:

> All my inner organs were upset, and the sensations of my
> body were no longer felt. For my consciousness had been
> transformed, as if I no longer knew myself, as if raindrops
> were falling from the Hand of God upon my soul.

Reading this passage sends shivers up and down my spine. Hildegard was obviously a medieval priestess in disguise.

The power of the female to stand her ground in the face of adversity is quite extraordinary. Rigoberta Menchu is a living example of this. Raised in a small town in Guatemala, Rigoberta witnessed the most appalling atrocities against members of her family who had dared to stand up to the government. She refused to be silenced even when her own life was threatened, and formed a powerful women's peace movement which caught the attention of the world when she won the Nobel Peace Prize in 1992. She now travels and lectures all over the world on ethnic people's rights. The sisterhoods that these women, and so many others, have formed throughout history in the name of justice and truth are an inspiration to us all. These women leave us a great legacy to continue their work, and draw on their courage to stand up and be counted in a world which is going through such challenging times.

Resonating with my heroines has been a powerful experience for me, especially when I have needed to emulate their tenacity to win through in spite of all kind of opposition. So, when the chips are down, find a heroine who represents the personal qualities you want to manifest in yourself to get you through. Or, if you want to accomplish something, find a historical or modern heroine who has already achieved your dream. Make a shrine to her, and call upon her spirit to give you help and support. She will become a great friend and companion in so many ways, and you may also find that she symbolically turns up in your life in the most unexpected manner. It is as if she becomes alive in you and around you.

## Forming Your Own Sisterhood

Many personal crusades have been responsible for bringing vital aid to people from different parts of the world in desperate need, and to provide a voice for those unable to speak for fear of reprisal. The response to the plight of the refugees from the former Yugoslavia is a prime example. Most of us want to help in some way and forming a sisterhood is one of the ways we can all contribute. This, after all, is how the Women's Institute came into being! Women gathered together, over tea, cake and gossip, to raise money for local charities as well as providing companionship for each other. Yes, the Women's Institute is in fact a coven in disguise! And great work they have done, too, over many years.

Forming a sisterhood is not just about raising money, or even fighting a cause – it is about bonding together to provide a safe place to be with one another. The traditional time to meet is during each full moon. These are known as *esbats* in the pagan religion which comes from the French *s'ebattre*, meaning to have a good time! Followers of the old ways usually gather together in covens consisting of thirteen members. The number 13 represents the occult power of the thirteen pagan moons and therefore the Goddess herself. However it is not necessary to meet as a coven of thirteen to form a sisterhood. The most important thing is to be with friends with whom you feel comfortable. Therefore you can make your sisterhood as intimate as you wish. It is, however, particularly special to meet at the full moon because of its traditional association with woman's magic.

## Woman's Magic and the Moon

Historically, the moon played an important role in woman's magic because it too was seen to work magic on the land. Through its monthly sojourns, the tides of the seas and rivers mysteriously rose and fell, and unlike the sun and the other constellations which stayed static, its cyclic movement constantly enacted the cycle of life, death and resurrection. Thus the moon became the focus of many indigenous creation stories. Because it has no light of its own, it was considered to be the place where dead souls resided, as well as representing the human psyche and the mysterious dark side of woman that no man can touch. Its constant changing phases were also affiliated with rainfall and the possibility of floods, particularly during the full moon phases. These rains provided the earth with fertility, and so the moon became synonymous with the gods and goddesses associated with fecundity and fruitfulness. In fact, women who wanted to bear children would sleep underneath the rays of the moon to become impregnated by them. The word *moon* is derived from the Sanskrit root *mami*, meaning *measure* (as in time spans). Since time and fate are woven together, the moon also became synonymous with the feminine crafts of spinning and weaving. Many tales were told of how a woman would call upon

the mystical powers of the moon as she spun powerful enchant-
ments and protective spells into the clothing and weaponry of
her lord or champion. Just as many stories also told of terrible
revenge and destruction being woven with deadly intent using
poisoned spindles.

It is impossible to move on before explaining the effect that
the moon had on the whole of humanity and why it became the
focal point of so many religions. Even the efforts of the Christian
fathers were unable to wipe out its mystical and magical effect on
both farming activities and the calendar itself. Great importance
was given to the phases of the moon because it was more
fortuitous to plant seeds during the moon's waxing phase when
the water content of the soil was building. Animals which were
born during this phase appeared to be more robust in health, and
certainly more juicy to eat when slaughtered before the full moon.
Fishermen were also more successful clamming, shrimping and
crabbing during this period. Yet it was also found that leaving
castration and the removal of horns until the waning phase of the
moon, produced much less bleeding. Julius Caesar, on the advice
of his astronomer Sosigenes, created our present solar calendar
which was modelled on an original Egyptian solar calendar.
Nevertheless, lunar calendars are still used today in many parts of
the world. The date of the Islamic new year regresses because the
moon's cycle is shorter than the solar year, and the Hebrew calendar is synchronised with the solar year by including a leap year
every nineteen years. The Christian calendar is also influenced:
Easter is always selected as the first Sunday following the full moon
after the spring equinox. So the essence of woman's magic is still
entwined in all the major religious celebrations today, as well as
our daily lives.

In all the old religions each full moon was given a name to
describe its part in the annual cycle of nature, with the thirteenth
(the magical blue moon which appears every two to three years)

being incorporated into other moon names. Some of the names are as magical as the moon herself. The following are taken from Native American Indian tradition:

| | |
|---|---|
| January | Moon of frost in a tepee |
| February | Moon when coyotes are frightened |
| March | Moon of the big clouds |
| April | Moon of grass appearing |
| May | Moon when the ice goes out of the river |
| June | Moon when the buffalo bulls are rutting |
| July | Moon when cherries are ripening |
| August | Moon of the ripening corn |
| September | Moon when the calves grow hair |
| October | Moon of the falling leaves |
| November | Moon of the snowy mountains in the morning |
| December | Moon of the long night |

The naming of these lunar months brings a sense of wonderment and connection with nature back into life. Naming of the full moons is something we could do as a simple ritual once a month. This acts as a reminder and record of what each month brings as part of life's mystical and magical experience.

It is a wonderful gesture to give your own name for the full moon to describe the quality of its energy as a focus for the evening. This can be done through a simple ritual as follows:

## Naming the moon ritual

Once you are gathered together, light a silver or white candle which represents the magical qualities of the moon. Sit together in a circle, link hands and then, in your mind's eye, call out to the magic of the moon to manifest in your mind. Ask for a symbol to appear to each one of you. As soon as you all feel complete, you can share your experiences with one another. Compare your experiences, and see if there are any synchronistic messages. Find a common theme which you all resonate with, and use that as the focal point of your meeting. Perhaps each of you could draw the symbol which appeared to you, and take turns to talk about it. Use these times together to be constructive and to learn from each other rather than falling into the trap of having a group moan or a downer on men! It is a wonderful feeling to expand your consciousness, and to have positive uplifting conversations with each other. You will leave feeling so much better about yourself.

You will find that your sisterhood evolves at its own pace. One group I attended for a considerable time was intimate and simple – we were all old friends who lived locally. When we first started, it was just a get-together to have supper, and a chat about spiritual matters. It then went on to develop into a very powerful healing circle.

We started our evenings by joining hands in a circle and opening up to the Goddess through a short invocation prayer. We then ceremonially lit two candles (2 is the number of the moon) together with some incense. Each one of us would then write down a list of what no longer served us in our lives, or emotional issues which we wanted to release. When everyone had finished, we drummed and chanted for a few minutes to raise the energy, and then each of us in turn would read out our list and then burn it in the flame of the candle. We would then write down our focus for the coming month, and again read this outloud to be witnessed. This was concluded with another short burst of drumming and chanting. Finally we gave hands-on healing to each other as well as absent healing to those whom we knew were in need, and concluded it with a healing ritual for the whole planet. Everyone brought food and drink to share afterwards, so we always had a good feast and a bit of a knees-up!

It's a nice idea to take turns to host your sisterhood in each other's houses, which takes the emphasis off just one person organising it. Alternatively it could be held in a special venue to which individual speakers or workshop leaders are invited. It very much depends on what you as a group wish to achieve, and how complicated you want to make it. Some women like to dress up as priestesses for the occasion; others don't.

The important thing is to provide a space to come together to share what's important, and to be witnessed and supported, especially when life changes are taking place. You will find that as your group continues it really will begin to take on a personality of its own, and remember that 'from little acorns, big trees do grow'.

## Support through the Sisterhood

Many women I know who have opened their hearts to woman's magic have, in the interim, suffered broken relationships. So many are struggling as single parents, juggling careers and finances – yet still holding firmly on to the banner of the Goddess. To stand up for what you truly believe in is not an easy path to take, but it is the women who are predominantly taking the bull by the horns and saying 'stop' to what no longer feels right and just. This is why the support of each other is important, not just for those times of emotional turmoil and stress, but also for moments of triumph and joy as well.

The sisterhood is therefore about loyalty and respect, and welcoming to anyone who needs help. It is about compassion and understanding towards other women who have closed their hearts to the magic, choosing to live in bitterness and resentment. It is also about finding that ultimate forgiveness for another woman guilty of emotional betrayal. Many 'best friends' have ended up in bed with the husband or partner of their friend. Embracing the sisterhood means that you have moved beyond these kinds of emotional dramas, and that you are willing to put your energy to better use than creating havoc down a cul-de-sac! Breaking free of emotional dependency is tough, but it has to be done if we are truly to embrace our feminine power. As long as we are yearning for the romantic dream, or believing that a knight in shining armour is somewhere out there, we are living a life of illusion, and we are a danger to ourselves. It is this illusion which makes us steal another woman's partner; hurls us into pits of lonely despair and bitterness because we believe love has passed us by; or numbs us out as we sit on the sidelines of life waiting for the game to start. We can all recognise these traits within ourselves.

Breaking free of emotional dependency does not mean we have to turn our backs on intimate relationships either. Far from it. It means that we are no longer prepared to settle for second best, or for being held back by a partner who is unable to provide the necessary support for us to do our God-given work. The call to service has to come first, and everything else then falls into place. It is about completely trusting the Goddess to have our best interests at heart, and to decide if it is more beneficial for us to be with a partner or to be on our own. This is not just about being in an emotional relationship; it is possible that we need a close working partnership with someone of the opposite sex to achieve what needs to be done. Divine duality is the ultimate force within the universe.

When we surrender our hearts to the Goddess in this way, the yearning does loosen its grip which gives room for other jewels to surface – particularly our creative genius and that wicked intuition! Intuition is the greatest natural gift a woman possesses and is our innate link with Great Mystery and life beyond the veil. The sisterhood is a place where we can share our other-worldly adventures, and support those who are seeking to make the link.

But I would give a word of warning about the phenomenon of channelling which seems to be taking the world by storm. The danger lies in either giving your power over to some unseen force or setting yourself up as some sort of guru or miracle healer. There's an awful lot of people out there professing to have all the answers. **Take care in choosing where to cast your pearls**. Always listen to your inner voice, and trust that *you* have the answers for yourself and **no one else**. By developing your own way of being and maintaining a strong personal integrity, you will automatically draw in other women who are resonating at your level. Your sisterhood therefore will become a really exciting part of your life which is both rich and rewarding.

This brings me to reiterating the importance for each one of us to accept that we are all expressions of the Goddess and that our personal contribution is vital if the consciousness of the world is to change. It is also important to realise that what may feel right to us as individuals may not be palatable to others. So be aware that your personal spiritual beliefs are for you and those who are in synch with them. We who follow the old ways are respectful of all kinds of religions and spiritual practices and there is nothing worse than someone attempting to force their own personal philosophies down your throat. It is not for us to criticise or malign, and I believe we have a lot to learn from each other, no matter who we are or what we believe in. Personally I have found it a wonderful experience to share my spiritual beliefs with those I trust and respect, which is why the sisterhood plays an important role in my life.

## Sisterhood on the Net

Sisterhoods are growing! The Internet is a wonderful resource for keeping in touch with what women are doing together around the world – be it fighting for human rights and combating sexual discrimination or just forming a network to talk with each other about things that matter. I find it really heartening that so many women are taking control of their own needs by establishing new educational avenues, providing safe houses for one another, publishing books, making films, taking care of legal and financial issues, promoting health and family issues and, among a whole host of other things, writing great songs: Yes! Sisters are indeed doing it for themselves.

I would like to end *Woman's Magic* with something uttered by Lord Buddha himself:

'Women are the gods, women are life . . .
be ever amongst women in thought.

May the blessing of the Goddess in the guise of woman's magic be upon us all!

For further information about the Hoffman Process please contact The Hoffman Institute, The Old Post House, Burpham, Arundel, BN18 9RH Tel: (01903) 889990, E-mail: tim@quadrinity.com

# Bibliography

*A Return to Love* Marianne Williamson (Thorsons 1992)

*A Woman's Book of Shadows* Elizabeth Brooke (Women's Press 1993)

*ABC of Witchcraft* Doreen Valiente (Hale 1994)

*Aspects of Astrology* Sue Tompkins (Element 1998)

*Book of Flowers, The* Kathleen Partridge (Jarrold Colour Publications 1997)

*Book of Friendship, The* Kathleen Partridge (Jarrold Colour Publications 1997)

*Book of Shadows* Phyllis Curott (Piatkus 1998)

*Callings* Gregg Levoy (Thorsons 1997)

*Celtic Tree Oracle* Liz and Collin Murray (Connections Book Publishing 1998)

*Complete Guide to Magic and Ritual, A* Cassandra Eason (Piatkus 1999)

*Complete Guide to Divination, A* Cassandra Eason (Piatkus 1998)

*Complete Guide to Psychic Development* Cassandra Eason (Piatkus 1997)

*Culpeper's Herbal Remedies* Dr. Nicholas Culpeper (Wiltshire Book Company 1980)

*Earth Power* Scott Cunningham (Llewellyn 1993)

*East Anglian Magic* Nigal Pennick (Hale 1995)

*Encyclopaedia of Gods* Michael Jordan (Kyle Cathie Ltd 1992)

*Encyclopaedia of Magical Herbs* Scott Cunningham (Llewellyn 1985)

*Enneagram, The* Karen Webb (Thorsons 1996)

*Enochian Magic for Beginners* Donald Tyson (Llewellyn 1997)

*Five Stages of the Soul, The* Harry R Moody and David Carroll (Rider 1997)

*Green Witchcraft* Ann Moura (Llewellyn 1997)

*Heal Your Body* Louise L Hay (Hay House Inc 1984)

# BIBLIOGRAPHY AND RECOMMENDED

*Herbal Magic* Scott Cunningham (Llewellyn 1984)

*Herbs for Cooking and for Healing* Donald Law PhD (Foulsham 1970)

*Higher Taste, The* (The Bhaktivedanta Book Trust 1984)

*Life Magic* Susan Bowes (Simon and Schuster 1999)

*Love Spells and Rituals* Sue Bowes (Thorsons 1998)

*Magick for Beginners* JH Brennan (Llewellyn 1998)

*Mythic Tarot, The* Juliette Sharman-Burke and Liz Greene (Eddison Sadd 1986)

*Notions and Potions* Susan Bowes (Thorsons 1997)

*Numbers Book, The* Sepharial (Foulsham 1957)

*Numerology: The Romance in Your Name* Juno Jordan (Devorss & Co 1965)

*Occult Properties of Herbs and Plants, The* WB Crow (The Aquarian Press 1980)

*Penguin Dictionary of Classical Mythology* Pierre Grimal (Penguin 1991)

*Planets in Transit* Robert Hand (Whitford Press 1976)

*Pot Pourri and Other Scented Delights* Reginald Peplow (Unwin Hyman 1987)

*Rodale's Illustrated Encyclopaedia of Herbs* (Rodale's Press 1987)

*Sacred Path Cards* Jamie Sams (HarperCollins 1990)

*Shamanism* Leo Rutherford (Thorsons 1996)

*The New Holistic Herbal* David Hoffman (Element 1986)

*Transformation Through Insight* Claudio Naranjo (Hohm Press 1997)

*Tree Wisdom* Jacqueline Memory Paterson (Thorsons 1996)

*Understanding the Tarot* Juliet Sharman-Burke (St Martin's Press 1998)

*World of Herbs, The* Lesley Bremness (Ebury Press in association with Channel 4 1990)

# Index

# INDEX